Bowperson's Guide To Racing:
Symmetrical Spinnaker Edition

A Technical Checklist Style Manual
By
Team Coordinated Racing

Dolphins are the epitome of
Team Coordinated when they hunt

Copyright ©2021 Team Coordinated Racing & the company's owner

Brand: **Team Coordinated Racing**

www.TeamCoordinatedRacing.com

"www." and capitalization optional for website

All rights reserved. This book or any portion thereof may not be reproduced or used in any manner whatsoever without the express written permission of the publisher except for the use of brief quotations in a book review.

ISBN: 978-1-7343572-0-2

Printed in the United States

First Edition, 2020

Front Cover Photo Taken by Erica Lowe by request of the owner of Team Coordinated Racing at his father's memorial sail

Front Cover Design Idea by Lillian Yao

Remembrance Photo Taken by Erica Lowe by request of the owner of Team Coordinated Racing at his father's memorial sail

All other photos taken by the owner or his family

Preface

I can happily say I represent a Jimmy Buffett song; I am a son of a son of a sailor. My grandfather was a member of Seal Beach Yacht Club from the first year it was created. He started racing sailboats and passed it down to my father early in his life. Three generations of my family have raced sailboats in and around Long Beach, California, a city with consistent racing wind year-round.

My father and mother both worked at schools and had summers free. My parents took me to Santa Catalina Island a few times as an infant on a Columbia 22. The first time was when my mother was 6 months pregnant. The second time was when I was 6 months old. As you can see my life has revolved around the ocean. My father bought a Catalina 27 when I was 3 years old to better fit the family. Additionally, my grandfather had a power boat and a mooring at Two Harbors, Catalina Island. We went several times each summer and a couple times each winter. We took the sailboat out most weekends in the summer even if we did not make the trip to the island.

My brother and I became quite adept at sailing. My father ran us through many tests prior to letting us take the boat out by ourselves. One test he drilled us on was throwing a cushion overboard randomly and saying "man overboard." We had to go back, stop the boat, and pick up the cushion ourselves while driving and trimming a 27 foot long sailboat with high gunwales. All the years on the water allowed me to develop a natural instinct to read the water and feel a boat responding under me.

My parents helped my twin brother and I earn the rank of Eagle Scout. We stayed active all the way through until the cutoff of age 18. I decided to race sailboats now that my weekends were free. Even with years of sailing experience I had to be taught how to race. There were a lot of new unique details. A person with the knowledge and ability to teach had to take me under their wing. It takes dozens to hundreds of races or practices to learn all the maneuvers.

My father, being a teacher, instilled in me techniques to reach people while teaching. Prior to racing, I taught several people two different events: pole vaulting and line dancing. These are fast-paced events that are not forgiving with the slightest mistake; later in my life, this would also describe racing.

After twenty years I have raced on all kinds of boats with all kinds of people. I have learned new details with each event, and I have used that knowledge to teach numerous people. A few years ago, while standing on the bow calling the line during an exhibition fleet race, I noticed all the other bowpeople were people that I had trained. Each was selected to do bow during this match racing regatta. That was incredible to know I had affected racing so much. A couple days later I remembered some of those people had not raced in a while prior to that event. I then wondered how well they did in their position having to perform without recent racing experience, and without my assistance. I questioned if they remembered some, most, or all the details I had passed on to them. This started my interest in writing down my knowledge. I wrote down bits and pieces over the years whenever someone I was teaching mentioned they liked learning from me or asked why I had not written things down. My kick in the pants came after my father passed. He was provided a burial at sea. His memorial was held at the US Sailing Center, in Long Beach, where he taught sailing at times.

This photo and previous photo are of Santa Catalina Island, Isthmus/Two Harbors and my father's power boat

Acknowledgments

In honor of my Father Cal "Butch" Macy

He is the reason I enjoy the ocean. He is the reason I enjoy racing so much. My dolphin brand picture logo is a photo he took while we were driving to Catalina. The above picture was taken the Wet Wednesday after he passed. In honor of him not being on the boat that night a black band and a "In Memory of" nameplate were on the boat. Below picture means he lives on teaching at the U.S. Sailing Center Long Beach on an appropriately named Cal 20.

Thanks to the amazing people who taught me bow:

Karen Campbell (boat: Joann); Steve Comstock (boats: Chayah, Catalina 37's); Linus Ralls (RIP)(boats: Catalina 37's, Temptress, Dark Star, many others)

Thanks to the skippers who got me out on the water:

Steve Murphy (Joann, Santana 30/30); Oscar Krinsky (Chayah, 1D45); Bob Marcus (Code Blue, Shock 35); Wes Selby (TNT, Trip 47); Mike Sego (Catalina 37's - Wet Wednesdays); Dave Hood (Catalina 37's - Wet Wednesdays, Long Beach Race Week, match racing); Ray Godwin (Temptress, Farr 40); Glenn Griley (Stampede, J120); Marty Vogel (Relentless, 1D35 turbo); several others; Steve Brown (Catalina 37's - Long Beach Race Week; Brown Sugar, Express 37; Dark Star, Farr 40); Jeff Busche (Catalina 37's - Wet Wednesdays); Paul Cassanova (Flaquitta, Reichel-Pugh 44); Phillip Friedman (Sapphire Knight, Farr Grand Mistral 88)

Thanks to those that helped me with this book:

my wife April; Lillian Yao; my brother Chris; Erica Lowe; Chris Doolittle; Mike Reed; Kurt Hanna; Nathalie Tessier; Christine DeLabre; the boats and people in my pictures; everyone over the years I taught who mentioned to write this down

Intro

When a group of people set out to race a sailboat they are usually called a crew. To me, that kind of feels like a group of people filming a movie. Buoy racing is a lot more fast paced and competitive than filming a movie. Coordinating the actions of four to six or more people is not an easy process! When that group of people works together to fulfill the positions and duties needed to get the boat around the race course, they become a team.

Racing sailboats not only requires physical effort, but a lot of mental effort. Both mental and physical effort can be reduced if a boat (1 - Is setup well for racing; 2 - Is well maintained; 3 - Has consistent team members). Once the boat leaves the dock these factors are for the most part in place. Your teamwork will be tested from then on out.

Many maneuvers need to be timed well to go smoothly. Planning and coordinating in advance is key for a team to be in sync. The smallest action done too early or too late causes repercussions throughout the boat; likely throughout the whole sequence of a maneuver. Clean maneuvers allow for less time, mistakes, energy exertion by teammates, and damage to the sails and boat. The boats that usually win regattas are the boats that have the fewest mistakes. Bow is one of the most important positions to not make a mistake in.

I strongly suggest everyone who races regularly to experience bow during a practice to know how much it is affected by others. I have performed and taught racing in all positions on the boat. I regularly instruct newer people at their positions while simultaneously doing bow. The bow position becomes a lot easier when maneuvers are coordinated properly with the back of the boat. I have written down my checklist of procedures and coordination items I go through every time I am on the water performing my duties as a bowperson. I have also included the checklist of procedures I perform to assist bow when performing another position on the boat.

A bowperson stands up on the narrowest part of a pitching boat while performing duties. Bow is responsible for the 'transitions;' the maneuvers performed during changes in direction while proceeding around a race course. A lot of the time when the bowperson makes a mistake it can lead to a major incident that highly reduces boat speed and takes valuable time to fix. Some things done by others can lead to a major incident that bow also has to fix. Accepting that the bowperson is usually the one held accountable is considered part of the duties. Most people who learn bow want to work their way towards the back of the boat due to this. Two common phrases come to mind: "Never do a bad job well," and "An unhappy bowperson means an unhappy boat." I feel that bow is the best position on the boat when the other positions are not doing things to make the bow team work harder.

This book is designed as a per position, per maneuver mental checklist. This book applies to a broad array of boats with the added ability to be referenced on the water. You can quickly look up things after you ask: "What went wrong?" or "What could we have done differently?" When reviewed prior to racing this book can save problems on the water. This book serves as a consistent set of procedures that when properly practiced provides coordination to assist the bow in preventing major incidents. It provides a checklist for consistent communication items and processes to use during maneuvers so you and your teammates can perform....

Team Coordinated Racing

Table of Contents

Bowperson's Guide To Racing:
Symmetrical Spinnaker Edition
Table of Contents

1. **Boat Prep**aration
2. **Personal Prep**aration
3. Racing **Positions**
4. Prestart & **Start**
5. **Upwind**
6. Windward **Set**
7. Gybe (**End for E**nd)
8. Gybe (**Dip** Pole)
9. **Leeward** Rounding
10. **Spin**naker Takedown

➢ Bow
○ Mast
▪ Pit
◇ Cockpit
❖ Main Trim
☐ Skipper
♪ Tactician

Table of Contents

Disclaimer: Sailboat racing is a dangerous sport. The information provided herein is for informational purposes only. Observe racing several times from the back of the boat prior to moving forward. Then have someone teach your desired position on the specific boat prior to stepping into that position. Safety is solely in your hands. Practice safe racing and race at your own risk. **Team Coordinated Racing** is not responsible in any way for injury or death.

A previous photo is of my father inside the L.A. lighthouse below

Los Angeles Lighthouse, 100 years old, shortly after being repainted

Boat Preparation

General

As mentioned previously the skipper has a lot of work to do prior to the boat leaving the dock. The team should help with maintenance, food, water, etc., as much as possible. Because the skipper is the reason that you can go out and have a fun time racing. The skipper must assure the boat is rigged, stocked and safe to race.

Unless you have a dedicated set of people regularly showing up having enough team members is sometimes harder than the maintenance. Email chains work best to have close to twenty people, because scheduling six to nine people is not easy. I have noticed that there is about a third dropout factor when recruiting team members; unless it is a major regatta everyone schedules in advance. To get nine people, arrange a team of twelve people two to three weeks in advance. Make sure you have team members with enough physical strength to handle their position for at least seventy-five percent of the whole regatta without struggling because physical fitness does come into play. People are more likely to get hurt or do something that hurts someone else when they get weak.

Another way to have a safe race is to consider the conditions. If wind or wave conditions are high it is a good time to consider the whole team putting on PFD's. Wearing a PFD is not something that should be scoffed at by others. When you have been racing long enough you realize that anything can happen at any time. If you cannot swim solidly for at least fifteen to thirty minutes with clothes, you should always wear your PFD. I personally feel it should be a requirement to wear a PFD with strobe and whistle at night. A personal E.P.I.R.B. is a good thing to have with each person on long distance races. It is highly recommended to wear a PFD in areas of extremely cold water. I know there are mixed opinions about whether to be tethered to the boat, so that is up to the race committee or each skipper.

Walk any people new to racing through safety items prior to leaving the dock. Ask the person what experience they have with sailing or racing and explain the basics of sailing if needed. Then teach them what is expected of them and where they will be throughout the race. Usually the back of the boat is the most secure for someone to watch and learn. Teach them to watch out for to following: person grindings handle and arms, a person tailings arms, pit person tailings arms, main sheet, jib sheet, getting fingers caught in winches, blocks or cleats including cams, etc. Introduce any new people during your safety meeting prior to

Boat Prep

leaving the dock. State their previous experience so that everyone on board will know to assist with that person's safety. Advise where life jackets are as well as man overboard throwables. Advise that the main thing is to stay on board, to not get hurt and to have fun. Ask the person's swimming strength and advise them to wear a life jacket if necessary. Explain to them that holding on is the best option but if they end up free of the boat the main problem with people going overboard is when they panic. Notify them to try to make a noise if they go in the water so that someone hears them. Notify them to wave their arms and ensure someone saw them. Stay calm and wait for the boat to return.

    Here are some recommended items to stock: enough food to keep strength up; enough water and electrolyte adding drinks to combat dehydration; all Coast Guard required safety devices; knife on deck to cut sail lines if boat gets out of control; chart of the area to ensure traveling in safe waters; harness to go up the mast; enough sails inventory in good condition to do the race, especially to handle high winds; extra lines, shackles, rings, blocks, etc.; tools; sail repair items; boat anchor; items to cut halyards and stays if the mast breaks and needs to be cut loose; boat hook; life raft; harness for going up the mast; radar deflector; bucket (can be used for bailing water or many other things); sponge; first aid kit; hand water pump; water bailer; folding swim ladder to retrieve people overboard; and red lights inside the cabin for night races.

A sunset in Huntington Beach
with Santa Catalina Island outline

Boat Prep

Personal Preparation

General

I learned I became better when I mentally walked my way through the steps as a precursor to racing. I learned that practice with repetition to set muscle memory so that the mind and body no longer fight each other as to what to do. A big trick I learned was to stop when you get to a part where you made a mistake. After you figure out the mistake, either start the whole process over, or do the item correctly and continue from there. Doing the process the wrong way does not help your body to form that muscle memory. Teaching made me realize there is no other way to become skilled at anything unless you do it the right way multiple times until it becomes natural. Showing and talking about it can help, but only gives an abbreviated perspective of the complex aspects involved.

Below are some bullet point items to follow to make yourself a better racer.

- know safety equipment locations and procedures to follow (PFD's, man overboard devices, radio, flares, etc.)

- enroll in trainings regarding boat handling and safety

- wear and bring proper racing equipment only. For example: shoes and gloves required, a pair of polarized sunglasses with keeper strap is highly recommended, sunscreen, clothing should not be cotton, all items should be able to get wet, Ultraviolet Protection Factor clothing to protect from the sun, bring clothing that can be layered to get warmer, all items should pack small

- harness if you go up the mast (to ensure your own safety)

- PFD with whistle, strobe, and possibly personal EPIRB

- cell phones put away

- chatter reduced to mainly race-related talking from 10 minutes before start

- red (or green) headlamp for overnight races

- know that all items you bring onto a boat may get damaged or lost

- learn common sailing and racing terms

- solidly know port and starboard

- solidly know tack versus gybe

- know common sailing knots: bowline, clove hitch, half hitch, figure eight

Personal Prep

- know how to secure a boat at the dock with dock lines

- know how to start and operate the boat you are on; this is also a safety factor

- sail and skipper small boats. the experience you get is super valuable

- recognize when a boat is tacking and perform the maneuver without the tactician having to call it

- ask questions. always try to learn more

- always make sure you know the maneuver you are performing prior. do not just assume you know what to do. doing a maneuver wrong is usually worse than not doing it

- stay out of the way of others if you do not know how to assist properly. unless someone explains clear enough for you to understand what to do

- be courteous to others

- no yelling unless a dangerous situation needs attention. you all have to be together for hours in a small space. remember everyone is trying to get out and have a good time

- concentrate on your position. as a bowperson I have found that usually the person who is the most vocal about me needing to do one of my tasks is the person keeping me from doing that because they are too busy directing another position and they are not doing their task as a result

- give advice stated that "the boat would do better if" a certain thing was done. refrain from mentioning a certain position

- directly giving advice to a person needs to be done delicately. be on the lookout for bad reactions, even if a prior conversation states someone is open to accepting criticism. word any advice as constructive criticism

- always act as if your suggestions for change are an option that may help but are open to discussion

- review procedures prior to each maneuver

- visualize procedures prior to maneuvers

- visualize possible issues and how to overcome them

- race on the same boat while learning each position

- know how you learn and memorize the procedures in this book (e.g. have someone read it to you, read it out loud yourself, write it down yourself, or whatever you need to do)

- dedicate yourself to a boat for a certain number of races and stick to your commitment

- ask your skipper to practice on a non- race day

- ask your skipper if you can take the helm for a few maneuvers during the practice

- practice man overboard at least once a season

- during practice take reefs in and out of the main

Personal Prep

- observe several times before taking on any new position
- observe a position for each boat you are on because there are differences
- only jump on other boats if you are confident you have a solid grasp of your position. you do not want to be having to put in effort to remember and perform the main steps, because slight changes needed for a different boat will take most of your effort
- make sure you help set up before the race
- make sure you help clean up after the race
- make sure you get feedback after racing. this is usually done with the whole boat debriefing
- make sure you have all the tools on the boat for the the position you are doing. marking sheets, halyards, boomvang, etc help for consistency for example. have all snub lines, temp blocks, etc ready for install
- take off rings before racing to keep them from having to be cut off if finger swells
- lock in your knowledge by teaching someone else
- compile your **Racing Resumes.**

see www.TeamCoordinatedRacing.com. these will help you grow, or campaign a new boat. "www." and capitalization optional for website.

    I hope you can use this book to learn multiple positions on the boat. The more you know, the better racer you will become.

    The bullet points in the maneuvers chapters are repetitious because it allows for "wrote memorization"

Personal Prep

Sunset on the water. One of the best things in life. Taken while doing a boat delivery from Los Angeles to San Francisco as a family. My brother, father and I.

Information: I am currently sole proprietor of **Team Coordinated Racing**. I have created a website and books in the sole interest of passing on my knowledge so that others may have the same fun on the water as I do. Printing and distribution costs have been kept low to try to keep the book affordable to you. I have tried to mimic the book that is most familiar to all racers, the one that provides the rules to sailboat racing. It is my hope that those wanting to hone procedures can use this book to do so with the straight forward information that has worked for many others prior.

Me inside Los Angeles Lighthouse

I got special access only because I was bidding to repaint it with the company I worked for at the time. I took my father along

Personal Prep

Positions

Racing Positions

General

All lines lead to the front of the boat. Thus, all eyes need to be looking forward watching how pulling something effects the front. The back and front of the boat need to be coordinated. High winds, noisy sails, waves, and other things make for a lot of noise isolating the bowperson from the back of the boat. The pit person is the relay back and forth. Tactician is best to coordinate timing by having a set of commands for each maneuver that provide cadence through the procedures. All jib and spinnaker sheets should be attached to a solid part of the boat so that any pull is on the boat. This can be a winch, temporary block, run through a pad eye, etc. All movements should be smooth to not bounce the boat.

Buoy racing is tough. Long Distance racing uses the same principles but allows for a lot more time to coordinate maneuvers. Wind can change direction and speed throughout the day. Racing in high winds is a dangerous thing and makes the timing of tasks even more critical because high wind causes high loads. Each position has specific tasks to perform to get the boat around the course safely. When multiple capable people are close together (bow & mast, or multiple cockpit people) the closest person should do the next thing needed. Switching positions takes time. Remember the people working together are a team; fighting to maintain all aspects of a certain position is not cooperation. Everyone works together to get the boat around the course.

The ideal is to keep consistent team members in the same positions over the course of a racing season. As explained previously, people are busy, so team members may change frequently. I realize all positions play critical parts in having a good race, but to have a safe race it is best to make sure you at least have experienced people in the positions of bow and pit. After that you should have at least one person in the cockpit, then mast, then main. The tactician is always going to have experience to be a safety factor to help the back of the boat. Usually the skipper too.

The positions to follow in this chapter list the critical components of each. I have a different bullet point for each position for easy reference in each chapter. Work to commit to knowledge your role on the boat, then skim the other positions to see how your position effects others on the boat.

Positions

Bow (part of the bow team)

➤ perform work on the most dangerous part of the boat. it is the most bouncy, wet, slippery, and narrow part of the boat, with the most lines and things going on around you. there are many ways to get hurt in this position; have a respect for that

➤ balance, speed, and attention to detail are needed

➤ endurance is needed to hoist and retrieve sails multiple times a race

➤ 70% 'preparation' where the little details matter.

15% 'perspiration' of quickly going through the procedures during the maneuvers.

15% 'experience' allowing for quick reactions to standard changes.

a great bowperson has an additional 10% of incident reaction and recovery knowledge

➤ most responsible for getting the boat around the corners. getting the sails up and down cleanly

➤ always double check to make sure the boat is setup for next possible maneuver. think out every step that would be advantageous for the next procedure. tell the pit what problems there may be ahead of time. **be prepared for anything**

➤ advise tactician of time frames of maneuvers

➤ accept or reject changes in procedures

➤ adapt maneuvers to the team's abilities, time required, and the weather conditions

➤ try to do as many items as possible as far aft as possible. the weight on the bow buries the bow and makes it harder for the skipper to steer the boat

➤ straighten and/or pack the spinnakers – I like to start at one side and run along the foot first then put the clews down onto the deck. then I run up to the head of the spinnaker. two sides clean means the third is automatically clean. this is called 'running the tapes'

➤ I like to put the foot on the bottom and head on top so it is easy to see the spinnaker triangle having no wraps before and during the hoist if doing hatch set

➤ keep morale up by giving praise to the team for items performed well; especially try to find things to be positive about when things go wrong

➤ know how to use bent knees and wide stances to absorb shock and keep balance

➤ know where your secure foot placements are. chines are best. I feel it is

Positions

best to place your foot with the outer edge of ball of your foot on the top of the chine. this angles your foot in toward the middle of the boat allowing for good push off. if you place your foot against the side of the chine you are more likely to roll your ankle when the boat shifts

➤ I always explain that in rough water bow is always in a state of 'controlled falling.' trying to do your tasks with your arms above your head does not allow for 'one hand for the boat.' the boat can angle heavily and sometimes quickly. a quick up and then down of the bow could cause you to lose contact with the boat. always know where you can quickly grab something, or jamb a limb into something to keep you on board if you start to lose your balance. you need to always know where the boat is, and if you start to fall, readjust to falling in the direction of the boat in a manner that will not hurt you. drop to one knee toward the center of the boat if needed. controlling how and where you fall is better than trying to fight it, because when you lose the fight you will likely get hurt or thrown overboard

➤ make sure to not get hit or wrapped up in any sheet or sail

➤ ensure mast, human guy, and squirrel know what to do and how to be safe

➤ watch for kelp, dangerous objects, obstructions and other boats

➤ depending on what the skipper and/or tactician like: call out wind puffs, call out big waves

➤ store the most heavily used halyards and topping lift where they can be accessed most easily. ones not used should be stored higher or behind the mast to avoid crossing lines

➤ walk forward with halyards and look up to ensure they are free before hooking them up every time

➤ realize that the team is working together to get the boat around the course as cleanly and fast as possible. if the mast person is capable and is at a spot to do the next thing that needs to be done, they do it

➤ anything that comes on deck MUST be tied down or attached to a line that will keep it from being lost if a wave hits it. some boats have bungie cords to stretch across the deck; these work great if not trapping any lines needed for maneuvers. spinnaker poles are expensive; spinnakers and jibs are too. I have seen a lot of jib bags go sliding off the deck because they were forgotten during a hoist. spinnaker bags will go flying if not clipped onto the lifeline prior to hoist

Mast (part of the bow team)

o endurance is needed to jump halyards multiple times a race

o read bow, pit, human guy, and squirrel descriptions here in <u>Racing Positions</u> so that you know generally what they do

Positions

o speed is needed

o balance is needed

o make sure to not get hit or wrapped up in any sheet or sail

Pit (part of the bow team)

▪ fast paced

▪ endurance is needed to hoist sails multiple times a race

▪ attention to detail is needed

▪ experience is needed: know what line does what. the more experience in the position the better. knows without much thought which line to pull when

▪ relay info back and forth from the bow to tactician. make sure the tactician and cockpit know their procedures in the next maneuver

▪ pit especially watches and does **ONLY** what the bowpeople are doing at the time. eyes forward whenever someone is in front of the mast!!

▪ do whatever is needed to minimize the bowperson's efforts. pit can actually fix problems to make the boat perform better. pit can delay releasing halyards, drop topper early or later, or many other things to correct minor problems that happen in the back of the boat. talk to or physically assist people in the back of the boat

▪ having a second person available is usually helpful during mark roundings

▪ keep fingers clear of winches. especially when adding or removing wraps from the winch

▪ keep fingers clear of deck blocks at all times

▪ keep fingers clear of cleats and / or cams used to secure halyards in place

▪ know which way to wrap the winches

Cockpit (1-4 people)

◇ at least 1 person with specific experience is needed

◇ know which way to wrap the winches

◇ trim the sails to the driver

◇ watch forward to ensure what you are doing is not hindering the bowperson

Positions

◇ listen, watch, and do what the bow needs done

◇ communicate with the driver on wind power in the sails

◇ attention to detail is needed

◇ concentration is needed for downwind trim

◇ keep fingers clear of winches. especially when adding or removing wraps from the winch

◇ keep fingers clear of deck blocks at all times

◇ keep your area clean and ready for next maneuver

◇ keep from getting wrapped up in sheets

◇ grinder turns the winch handle as fast as possible while looking at what is being ground in and listening to the trimmer. jib grinding starts just as the jib is released. jib trimmer may need grinder to stay and do more grinding. jib trimmer will call out "go to high side" when done. be ready and jump into place when you hear "prepare to tack." spinnaker grinding is done when the spinnaker trimmer calls "grind;" go until you hear "stop"

◇ jib trimmer tails as fast as possible while looking at what is being ground in to make sure everything is going okay. listens for any calls for assistance that may require not pulling in on the jib. instructs the grinder on when to stop grinding. may need grinder to stay and do more grinding. when done with grinder call out "go to high side." finish final trim and head to high side if possible. listen and be ready to assist skipper and adjust jib. be ready and jump into place when you hear "prepare to tack." jib trimmers may trim both sides or always on starboard or port side. port side is usually where you want the more experienced person because you have right of way on starboard you are more likely to be on that board when maneuvering for position at the start

◇ the person who 'cuts' releases the jib sheet to allow it to tack. will be the same person every time if jib trimmer does both sides

◇ spinnaker trimmer adjusts the spinnaker sheet and makes sure the spinnaker is full. usually stands in a position they can see the sail. is constantly looking at the sail. can pull strongly when needed. usually one person does spinnaker trim the whole race for consistency. notifies the grinder when to "grind" or "stop." may free-fly the spinnaker by themselves

◇ afterguy person adjusts the location of the pole fore and aft. may help with the spinnaker sheet on that side while free-flying the spinnaker. this will be prior to the pole being "made" and the transfer to the afterguy

Positions

Main trim

❖ work with Skipper to keep the boat in control

❖ the main is like a car's gas pedal

❖ ease the main if the boat heals over too much because the boat is not as efficient through the water

❖ ease the main if the boat has too much "weather helm." meaning the boat is automatically turning upwind. the rudder is a big surface that creates drag when the skipper has to fight weather helm

❖ strength is needed

❖ concentration is needed

❖ keep fingers clear of winches. especially when adding or removing wraps from the winch

❖ check to make sure batten tension is accurate

❖ control gybes by grinding in the main sheet prior

❖ make sure everyone is clear of the main sheet prior to gybes

❖ if controlling a gybe by a hand on the main sheet make sure you have firm footing. know that a release is needed to keep from being pulled onto the deck hard or pulled overboard

❖ know which way to wrap the winches

Skipper

□ state each person's racing position while driving out to the race course

□ keep the boat under control and perform maneuvers according to the abilities of the team

□ drive 'fast'

□ <u>drive</u> as close to dead <u>downwind</u> as you can, known as 'DDW', <u>if trouble with spinnaker up. dead upwind if trouble with jib up</u>

□ know the 'Racing Rules of Sailing'

□ <u>concentrate solely on driving</u>. do not look at anything that does not assist driving safely and fast in the correct direction. let the team do their positions

Positions

Tactician

♪ watch the wind and the other boats then direct maneuvers to go the best direction on the course

♪ adapt maneuvers to the team's abilities, time required, and the weather conditions

♪ coordinate with the bow and the rest of the boat as to the maneuvers being done. use the pit as the relay

♪ call out a series of commands to create a cadence for maneuvers

♪ keep morale up by giving praise to the team for items performed well. especially try to find some stuff to be positive about if things are going bad

♪ know the race 'Sailing Instructions'. know the details regarding: times, upwind or downwind finish, any restricted areas on the course, or whether crossing through start line after the start is restricted, etc.

♪ have course chart and radio

♪ get the course and tell bow what it is

♪ check projected wind and sea conditions

♪ make sure rigging tension is set properly for projected wind speed for the day

♪ know local conditions of the race area: areas of more or less wind or current, shallow areas, etc.

♪ know the 'Racing Rules of Sailing'

Floater (only mentioned here)

• experienced person that helps in whatever way needed. usually pre-arranged items per maneuver. is there when stuff goes awry. is there to provide another hand to do something for someone who is too busy doing something else

• may do spinnaker retrieval from inside the boat if spinnaker going down a hatch. some call this squirrel or sewer. see description here in Racing Positions

• if already have a squirrel then helps with spinnaker take down from on the deck if needed. always know where the hatch is on the boat to keep from falling into the hole

• may act as a human guy holding the sheet out to keep the sail full when the pole is removed prior to spinnaker takedown. see description here in Racing Positions

Positions

Backstays (only mentioned here)

- if boat is equipped, releases and tightens the backstays accordingly making sure at least one is on to keep the rig standing. this is especially important upwind

- work with skipper and main trim to adjust tension

- keep fingers clear of winches. especially when adding or removing wraps from the winch

- know which way to wrap the winches

Rail Weight (only mentioned here)

- move from side to side quickly, and safely without getting in anybody's way

- does not try to assist unless you are 100% sure you know what you are doing. avoid causing issues by being in the way or doing something that should not have been done

- in lighter wind assists with 'roll tacks'

Squirrel (only mentioned here)

- goes down below and helps takedown the spinnaker

- go down below as late as possible to keep the weight out of the bow. usually tactician or bow tells you to. or you can tell because the bow team is about to raise the jib

- let bow or mast open the hatch

- you should not reach out and grab anything. everything should be handed directly to you. or pulled down because it is an afterguy or a spinnaker tape you are running

- bow or mast may hand you the afterguy to pull on during the takedown. leave slack on it until you hear "blow the sheet." pull the afterguy until you get to the clew. leave the clew and any afterguy slack on deck. I usually stand up and pull as hard as I can as fast as I can until I get to the clew. I then set the clew on the deck, pull the afterguy slack on deck, then grab the foot of the spinnaker and quickly sit down, this pulls a bunch in

- if you are not handed an afterguy you will have to wait until the foot of the spinnaker is handed to you

- pull on anything handed to you as fast as you can until you cannot pull anymore

Positions

- if another spinnaker tape is visible and able to be pulled on pull on that until you take up all the slack and cannot pull anymore

- throw the foot of the sail towards the side of the boat the spinnaker is being taken down on

- throw the aft spinnaker tape aft as you pull down on it

- throw the forward spinnaker tape forward

- ensure the jib sheet or any other sheets are not pulled in

- ensure you are not pulling on portions of the spinnaker that are over the pole

- continue pulling on portions of the spinnaker until you see that the clews and head are sitting just outside the hatch

- make sure bow no longer needs you. close the hatch if bow or mast has not done so

- straighten and / or pack the spinnakers – I like to start at one side and run along the foot first. then put the clews down onto the deck. then run up to the head of the spinnaker. two sides clean means the third is automatically. this is called 'running the tapes'

- head to the rail as soon as possible

Human Guy (only mentioned here)

- assists with spinnaker control when the pole is not hooked up. or when pole has been removed. always know where the hatch is on the boat to keep from falling into the hole

- hold the spinnaker sheet on the windward side where the pole typically would be hooked up. hold it down to keep the spinnaker from raising or bouncing or moving back and forth a lot. hold it to keep the spinnaker from going passed the headstay

- pole is removed during poleless sets, or gybes, or preparation for spinnaker takedown

Positions

Previous picture is of a sunset on the water. To me there is nothing more incredible! I highly recommend doing at least one overnight delivery, trip, or race to experience one.

To see pictures in color go to my website

www.TeamCoordinatedRacing.com

Links to my Facebook page and groups are on the "About" page. I am continually adding new racing related info on Facebook.

Heading to the race course of L.B. Midwinters 2019 on Dark Star on a Sunday the racing was actually cancelled due to extreme wind. Notice this is just main alone, no jib.

Prestart & Start
(and before start sequence)

General

See Chapter 1 Boat Preparation

See Chapter 2 Personal Preparation

Some Information in Chapter 3 Racing Positions

Some Information in Chapter 5 Upwind

Team Procedures

1. safety briefing
2. make sure everyone knows their position
3. prepare or reset boat and sails, including spinnaker
4. make sure everyone has eaten and hydrated
5. hoist jib
6. setup jib cars, inhaulers, halyard tension for good sail shape
7. practice tacking
8. practice spinnaker set, gybes, and takedown
9. stay out of the way of the tacking or gybing boom
10. observe as much about the weather as possible
11. observe as much about the course as possible
12. back down before the sequence
13. turn off motor and set the propeller
14. get countdown timers set to start sequence
15. perform prestart maneuvers for positioning
16. watch for hazards
17. start the race
18. setup for next tack
19. distribute weight properly

Bow

➤ ensure mast, human guy, and squirrel know what to do and how to be safe. these are usually the positions less experienced people are at. pit is part of bow team, but should know what to do, it is a critical position (1. safety briefing)(2. make sure [bow team] knows their position)

3. prepare or reset boat and sails, including spinnaker

➤ preparation is key – halyards not crossed and stored in proper locations. sail tapes ran, especially between races. sails packed or folded well. sail locations are known for quick access. all lines lead properly

Start

➤ reset the boat between races. all halyards, sails, and lines clean and in their proper place and attached

➤ if the jib is on deck in the bag, make sure that the bag is closed and tied to the boat. keep the bag tied until you remove it from the deck

➤ when heading out to the race course, do not hook up the jib halyard until ready to hoist the jib unless you have a fraculator line to keep the sail from running up the headstay early

➤ do not run the zipper pull off the end of the zipper until you are ready to pull the sail out of the bag. run the zipper back if you have enough time because it saves time later

➤ if jib bag is opened, hook up the jib tack to keep it from being lost overboard

➤ keep a sail tie with you during racing, unless the boat has bungie cords. you can tie the jib down to the deck to keep it from going overboard after lowering it

➤ 4. <u>make sure [bow team] has eaten and hydrated</u>

➤ 5. <u>hoist jib</u>

➤ 7. <u>practice tacking</u>

➤ 8. <u>practice spinnaker set, gybes, and takedown</u>

➤ 9. <u>stay out of the way of the tacking or gybing boom</u>

➤ 12. <u>back down before the sequence.</u> when the boat is head to wind hold the foot of the sail forward to keep it from flapping around

➤ have a watch with the correct countdown time to help facilitate direction of travel needed based on distance to start line versus time left (14. <u>get [your] countdown timer set to start sequence</u>)

   15. <u>perform prestart maneuvers for positioning</u>   &

   16. <u>watch for hazards</u>

➤ stand on the bow for best view

➤ notify mast they skirt the jib in tacks until after the start

➤ instinctively know who has the right of way and which way to tell skipper to turn to keep out of trouble

➤ notify your skipper if they can turn if you are coming up to a situation where the skipper may want to turn but a boat is nearby. swing your open hand back and forth to state there is room to swing. hold up a fist if a collision would happen. this is known as 'calling overlap'

➤ ensure the tactician sees boats that are needed to be seen by calling back "see __ boat?" this relates to boats hidden under the jib, boats on a collision course, or boats which have right of way

➤ keep an eye out for hazards on and in the water and call out to back of the boat course corrections to miss. preferably "up" during upwind and "down" during downwind

➤ call out "starboard" or any other directive to boats only when about to collide. the tactician usually calls this. it is best to count out loud after, "one-one thousand, two-one thousand, three-one thousand." this proves room and opportunity

➤ call out the distance to the start line with clear hand signals agreed upon prior to the race. know at all times where the start line is relative to the bow of the boat. getting a visual reference on land helps, but remember if the line is not perpendicular to the reference it will move as you run the line.

➤ hold up the number of fingers as distance in boat lengths from the line

➤ a fist out level with the water with pointer finger hooked out and down means half a boat length to the line

➤ a fist straight up is 'hold.' give a little extra space to allow for wiggling and delay of the reaction by the skipper. call "on the line"

➤ a thumb down means a part of the boat is passed the start line

➤ usually proceed to high side rail after race start or as soon as you can. you can go before the start if you know you are not going to have issues with other boats or being over the line (17. start the race)(19. distribute [your] weight properly)

Mast

3. prepare or reset boat and sails, including spinnaker

○ assist the bowperson as much as possible with preparations

○ assist the bowperson as much as possible as it requires a lot of energy consumption just to stand on a bouncing and typically tilted bow

○ assist bow with hauling on deck and hooking up headsails, especially during sail changes. bow needs the help to conserve energy

○ between races assist bow with resetting the boat. all halyards, sails, and lines should be clean and in their proper place. bow needs the help to conserve energy

○ jump the jib halyard (5. hoist jib)

7. practice tacking &

15. perform prestart maneuvers for positioning

○ during tacks stay out of what I consider the 'danger triangle.' this is the area between the mast and the hatch. this is the place where the jib clew with metal ring and jib sheets flap in the wind. you can stay at the middle

Start

of the hatch forward or stay behind the protection of the mast and shrouds

o mast skirts the jib during this time because the bow is busy. pull it in over lifeline. usually crosses under the jib on the bow during tacks or gybes holding the foot

o help pit relay info back and forth to bow

o skirt the jib if the back of the boat calls for it, but you should already do it and not need it called

o 8. <u>practice spinnaker set, gybes, and takedown</u>

o 9. <u>stay out of the way of the tacking or gybing boom</u>

o 19. <u>distribute [your] weight properly</u>, usually you head to the rail as soon as possible

Pit

3. prepare or reset boat and sails, including spinnaker

▪ pre-mark the pole height for spinnaker set and gybe

▪ pre-mark all halyards so that you can assure proper tensions

▪ work with main trimmer to get boom vang, and usually outhaul and cunningham set properly

▪ help bow with spinnakers and jibs before, during, and after the race

▪ relay info back and forth to bow

▪ raise jib and make sure halyard tensions are good (5. <u>hoist jib</u>)

▪ run your hand over the whole length of the jib halyard and loosely drop it where you desire it to stay to make sure it is clear for the takedown

▪ a lot of times pit is the one calling out time left in start sequence because does not have anything to do during this. plus, both front and back can hear (14. <u>get [your] countdown timer set to start sequence</u>)

7. practice tacking &

15. perform prestart maneuvers for positioning

▪ watch to make sure lazy jib sheet has enough slack in tacks

▪ 8. <u>practice spinnaker set, gybes, and takedown</u>

▪ 9. <u>stay out of the way of the tacking or gybing boom</u>

▪ 19. <u>distribute [your] weight properly</u>, usually you head to the rail as soon as possible

Cockpit

3. prepare or reset boat and sails, including spinnaker

◇ responsible for the sails you will be trimming: help bow ensure spinnakers are packed and stowed properly, ensure the jibs are ready to go, check jib batten tensions, help flake jibs when done with them

◇ make sure you have marks on sheets and spreaders to trim based on, including marks on afterguys to give enough slack for gybes

◇ always listen for people calling out for assistance needed

◇ always keep an eye forward when pulling or releasing something

◇ make sure the correct sail for the current wind conditions is up

◇ 6. setup jib cars, inhaulers, halyard tension, [etc.], for good sail shape

7. practice tacking

◇ coordinate who does what

◇ coordinate where people are crossing to get to the high side

◇ coordinate sitting position on windward rail. usually everyone returns to the same position every time

◇ coordinate when people get off the rail to prepare for the tack. the more people on the rail the longest is best

◇ practice tacks to make sure each person knows their role

◇ 8. practice spinnaker set, gybes, and takedown

◇ 9. stay out of the way of the tacking or gybing boom

15. perform prestart maneuvers for positioning

◇ keep the jib adjusted accordingly no matter what the skipper is doing

◇ call out for "skirt" if needed. jib to be pulled over lifelines

◇ know where the proper upwind full trim location is for the sail. judge by distance to the spreader or by distance inside the spreader. tape lines can be added on the spreader

◇ have enough wraps of jib sheet on the winch to not have to hold the main portion of the pressure on the sails. but not too many or you could cause an override

◇ know how to clear an override. usually you just need to grind it out. but sometimes you have to pull the slack side

◇ watch for loops that could stop the jib sheets from paying out through deck blocks. tug hard on the loose sheet until the loop comes out

Start

◇ unwrap the winch all the way when releasing the jib by pulling the sheet straight up from above the winch

◇ ensure the jib and sheets do not get snagged. clear the things you can. ask for assistance from bow team if needed

◇ listen to the tactician or skipper call out direction of travel desired so you can ease or bring in the sail accordingly

◇ a lot of the times sail is out to depower the boat prior to the start. be prepared for big grind and skirt to get the sail in and the boat up to speed quickly just before the start (17. start the race)

◇ prepare for the next tack by wrapping the lazy winch and putting the handle in. leave slack to not hurt the jib. make sure the sheet is on the winch the correct way (18. setup for next tack)

◇ 19. distribute [your] weight properly, usually you head to the rail as soon as possible

Main Trim

2. make sure [you] know [your] position

❖ know how to work the main trim and fine tune if equipped

❖ know how to work the main traveler

❖ make sure batten tension is proper before hoisting the main

❖ help hoist and fold the main

❖ know what the proper full trim of the sail looks like upwind, have marks on items you can to help with consistent trim: outhaul, boomvang

❖ make sure halyard tension, outhaul, boom vang, cunningham, backstays (if applicable), etc. are all set properly for good sail shape (3. prepare or reset boat)

❖ look at the bend in the mast up the forestay, as well as up each side of the mast

❖ make sure everyone 9. stay[s] out of the way of the tacking or gybing boom and main sheet

7. practice tacking   &

8. practice spinnaker set, gybes, and takedown   &

15. perform prestart maneuvers for positioning

❖ keep the sail flying properly and the boat moving fast no matter what the skipper is doing

❖ usually keep the sail at 90 degrees to the wind downwind

❖ look out to make sure everyone has their heads down during tacks and gybes

❖ for gybe details see gybe chapters following: end for end, or dip pole

❖ depower the main when skipper needs to duck another boat

Skipper

1. [perform] safety briefing [while at dock or heading out to course]

☐ remind everyone shoes required (I have to reiterate)

☐ may make the call for life vests required if at night or high winds or seas

☐ 2. make sure everyone knows their position

☐ 3. [make sure they] prepare or reset boat and sails, including spinnaker

☐ 4. make sure everyone has eaten and hydrated

☐ 5. [call for] hoist jib

☐ 6. [make sure they] setup jib cars, inhaulers, halyard tension for good sail shape

☐ 7. practice tacking

☐ 8. practice spinnaker set, gybes, and takedown

☐ 9. stay out of the way of the tacking or gybing boom

☐ 10. observe as much about the weather as possible

☐ 11. observe as much about the course as possible

☐ 12. back down before the sequence

☐ 13. turn off motor and set the propeller

☐ 14. [make sure they] get countdown timers set to start sequence

    15. perform prestart maneuvers for positioning

☐ drive the boat as smooth and safe and fast as possible while working with the tactician

☐ notify main trimmer if adjustment needed based on the feel of the helm

☐ talk with cockpit about sail trim – i.e.: need an ease to fall off the wind, need an ease to reach, set sails and head to high side, etc.

☐ turn boat at a proper speed – too fast of a turn does not allow enough time for jib to be pulled in

☐ 16. watch for hazards [ahead only]

☐ 17. start the race

Tactician

♪ 1. [make sure skipper performs] safety briefing

♪ 2. make sure everyone knows their position

   3. [make sure you and they] prepare or reset boat and sails, including spinnaker

♪ make sure the rig is tuned for the wind predictions

♪ read S.I.'s for: times, upwind or downwind finish, any restricted areas on the course, or whether crossing through start line after the start is restricted, etc.

♪ have course chart

♪ VHF radio tuned to race committee listening to anything they state

♪ 4. make sure everyone has eaten and hydrated

♪ 5. [make sure they] hoist jib

♪ 6. [make sure they] setup jib cars, inhaulers, halyard tension for good sail shape

♪ notify everyone of "prepare to tack / gybe," then "tacking / gybing." make sure everyone has their head down (7. practice tacking)

♪ 8. practice spinnaker set, gybes, and takedown

♪ 9. [make sure everyone stays] out of the way of the tacking or gybing boom

♪ know wind angles and speeds (10. [part of] observe as much about the weather as possible)

♪ 10. observe as much about the weather as possible

♪ 11. observe as much about the course as possible

♪ 12. [make sure they] back down before the sequence

♪ 13. [make sure they] turn off motor and set the propeller

♪ 14. get [your] countdown timer set to start sequence

♪ remind the boat 10 minutes before the start to keep noise to a minimum

15. perform prestart maneuvers for positioning

♪ get course from committee boat prior to start and tell bow what it is. then coordinate with bow what procedures predicted to be done

♪ guide skipper to best starting position and speed

♪ communicate with skipper which part of the line aiming for

♪ know length of time to the line

♪ watch bowperson's hand signals

♪ communicate with other boats as needed: starboard, tack or cross, come up, overlap, etc… it is best to count out loud after, "one-one thousand, two-one thousand, three-one thousand." this proves room and opportunity (16. [part of] watch for hazards)

♪ 16. watch for hazards

♪ 17. start the race

♪ advise everyone on the boat of the plan prior to maneuvers, not just skipper. remember to notify of any changes to previously made plans, especially last-minute ones

♪ 18. [make sure they] setup for next tack

♪ 19. [coordinate how to] distribute weight properly

I always train people learning mast or bow to stay out of the "Danger Triangle" when the jib is up. This is the area where the jib clew and sheets will be flapping around in the wind violently. Stay behind the mast and / or shrouds for protection or in front of the hatch for the best protection.

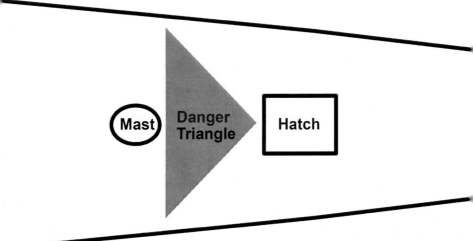

Start

Catalina 'Cat' Harbor, the backside of Two Harbors / Isthmus.
I have named this photo 'Cat Harbor Serenity"

Palos Verdes Peninsula with kelp forest.
Catalina can be seen if you look close enough on the right.

Upwind

General

Some Information in Chapter 1 <u>Racing Positions</u>

Some Information in Chapter 2 <u>Prestart & Start</u>

Team Procedures

1. coordinate in advance
2. tack upwind
3. stay out of the way of the tacking boom
4. distribute weight properly
5. reset spinnaker if after a leeward rounding
6. make sure nothing is dragging in the water
7. watch for hazards
8. prepare for windward set

Bow

➢ 1. <u>coordinate in advance</u>. mast no longer skirting jib

   2. <u>tack upwind</u>

➢ cross in front of mast under the jib during tacks, preferably holding the foot of the jib and assisting it around the mast and inside the lifelines

➢ stay out of what I consider the 'danger triangle.' this is the area between the mast and the hatch. this is the place where the jib clew with metal ring and jib sheets flap in the wind. you can stay at the middle of the hatch forward or stay behind the protection of the mast and shrouds

➢ skirt the jib if the back of the boat calls for it. but you should already do it and not need it called

➢ ensure the pole is stowed in a manner it will not go overboard or get hung up on anything. hook it up to something

➢ 3. <u>stay out of the way of the tacking boom</u>

   4. <u>distribute weight properly</u>

➢ you usually get on the rail as soon as possible

➢ check whether the bow is burying or not. move weight forward or aft accordingly

➢ 5. <u>reset spinnaker if after a leeward rounding</u>. if after a leeward mark rounding, you need to prepare for another spinnaker set. try to wait for the best possible time to get off the rail. wait until: everyone else is on the high side, you are not competing with another boat, no big waves, etc.

➢ 6. <u>make sure nothing is dragging in the water</u>

<u>7. watch for hazards</u>

➢ keep an eye out for hazards on and in the water and call out to the back of the boat course corrections to miss the object, preferably turning up during upwind. notify mast of any objects seen in the distance because two sets of eyes should ensure you do not lose it

➢ call out "starboard" or any other directive to boats only when you are about to collide. the back of boat usually calls this. it is best to count out loud after, "one-one thousand, two-one thousand, three-one thousand." this proves room and opportunity

➢ provide hand signals for direction of travel needed to safely allow a boat to cross in front. allow plenty of room because wind gusts could cause a decent amount of round up. I was recently involved in an accident that happened just because of this

<u>8. prepare for windward set</u>

➢ spinnaker on deck prior to arriving at windward mark. clip both bag clips to lifeline decently far forward. ensure you are not trapping any needed lines. preferably do this on a tack where you are not working under the jib

➢ spinnaker sheets and afterguys hooked up on the correct side of the boat with the pole on the opposite side of the boat prior to leeward mark rounding

➢ on the last upwind where the spinnaker is not under the jib, hook up spinnaker halyard if not hooked up prior to racing. tape or Velcro the halyard forward so it does not get caught on the jib, mast, or spreaders

➢ discuss with back of the boat procedure to set the spinnaker

Mast

○ know where you will be heading across the boat during tacks. bow is now responsible for skirting the jib (1. <u>coordinate in advance</u>)

<u>2. tack upwind</u>

○ stay out of what I consider the 'danger triangle.' this is the area between the mast and the hatch. this is the place where the jib clew with metal ring and jib sheets flap in the wind. you can stay at the middle of the hatch forward or stay behind the protection of the mast and shrouds

○ <u>make sure jib gets across without hanging up. you can bump the jib with the palm of your open hand to not get your fingers caught</u>

○ 3. <u>stay out of the way of the tacking boom</u>

4. distribute weight properly

o you usually get on the rail as soon as possible

o in lighter wind assist with roll tacks

o 7. watch for hazards. help keep an eye out for hazards on and in the water. preferably only tell the bow so bow can notify skipper if needed. preferably turning up during upwind. notify bow of any objects seen in the distance and keep watch on it because two sets of eyes should ensure you do not lose it

8. [help bow] prepare for windward set

o get the spinnaker from down below and hand it to bow on deck

o make sure bow hooks up the halyards and the sheets

Pit

2. tack upwind

▪ watch to make sure lazy jib sheet has enough slack in tacks

▪ 3. stay out of the way of the tacking boom

4. distribute weight properly

▪ you usually get on the rail as soon as possible

▪ in lighter wind assist with roll tacks

▪ relay information back and forth from bow to stern (2. tack upwind)(8. [part of] prepare for windward set)

▪ 8. prepare for windward set. make sure you and bow know the procedure to set the spinnaker

Cockpit

1. coordinate in advance   &

2. tack upwind

◇ coordinate who does what

◇ always listen for people calling out for assistance needed

◇ always keep an eye forward when pulling or releasing something

◇ have handle out of winch early before each tack. make sure to stow it properly to not lose it overboard

Upwind

◇ have enough wraps of jib sheet on the winch to not have to hold the main portion of the pressure on the sails. too many could cause an override

◇ keep fingers clear of winches, especially when adding or removing wraps from the winch

◇ keep fingers clear of deck blocks at all times

◇ release the jib just as the sail first begins to depower prior to the first flop like it does when the boat is head to wind. to release the jib on the soon to be lazy side is to 'cut'

◇ watch for loops that could stop the jib sheet from paying out through deck blocks

◇ unwrap the winch all the way when releasing the jib by pulling the sheet straight up from above the winch

◇ grinder has a solid stance over the winch in a manner which cannot be knocked over and pretty much directly over the handle

◇ grinder makes wide elbow swings, grinding fast, starting just after the cut of the other side sheet

◇ grinder listens and looks as much as possible for any issues that may arise. grinding while the sail is stuck could rip the sail. grinding when someone is wrapped up in a jib sheet is very bad

◇ grinder and final trimmer know how to use the different speeds of a winch if applicable

◇ grinder assists the jib into a certain place and runs to the high side rail. usually by a call from the final trimmer of "go high"

◇ grinder may have to jump off the rail or reach back and hold the tail of the jib sheet if final trimmer needs assistance

◇ 'tailer' pulls full arm lengths of sheet until sail is under pressure. also known as pulling with 'big arms.' hold the line taught and pull the grindings

◇ final trimmer adjusts to full trim and proceeds to high side if not going to do any direction changes

◇ in lighter wind the place where the grinder stops is held for a bit until the boat comes up to speed, then the final trimmer adjusts to full trim

◇ call out for "skirt" if needed

◇ prepare for the next tack by wrapping the lazy winch and putting the handle in. leave slack to not hurt the jib. make sure the sheet is on the winch the correct way

◇ keep lines cleaned up as much as possible. messiness allows for loops to form, which can get caught in blocks or worse, around somebody's foot

◇ 3. <u>stay out of the way of the tacking boom</u>

◇ 4. <u>distribute [your] weight properly</u>, usually you head to the rail as soon as possible

◇ make sure spinnaker sheets are not dragging in the water and slack taken back. especially after spinnaker takedown (5. <u>reset spinnaker if after a leeward rounding</u>)(6. <u>make sure nothing is dragging in the water</u>)

◇ 8. <u>prepare for windward set</u>. make sure you and bow know the procedure to set the spinnaker

Main Trim

2. tack upwind

❖ ensure proper full trim

❖ release one traveler and set the other side (now high side) while going through head to wind

❖ communicate with skipper about helm feel

❖ make sure everyone 3. <u>stay[s] out of the way of the tacking boom</u> and main sheet

❖ in lighter wind, keep the sail out a bit at first and then bring it in to full trim once the boat is up to speed

❖ depower the main when the skipper needs to duck another boat

Skipper

2. tack upwind

□ drive the boat as smooth, safely and fast as possible while working with the tactician

□ drive by telltales with the jib set to full trim

□ notify main trimmer if adjustment is needed based on the feel of the helm or desired direction change

□ talk with cockpit about sail trim (i.e.: need an ease to fall off the wind, need an ease to duck another boat, set sails and head to high side, etc.)

□ 3. <u>stay out of the way of the tacking boom</u>

□ drive the proper amount of degrees with the jib set to full trim. inform cockpit if you need to go a specific direction so they can trim accordingly

□ turn the boat at a proper speed – too fast of a turn does not allow enough time for jib to be pulled in

□ 7. <u>watch for hazards [ahead only]</u>

□ listen to calls from the bow about course changes needed

Tactician

♪ 1. <u>[make sure they] coordinate in advance</u>

    2. <u>tack upwind</u>

♪ notify everyone of "prepare to tack," then "tacking." make sure everyone has their head down

♪ work with skipper to choose optimal route to windward mark

♪ 3. <u>[make sure they] stay out of the way of the tacking boom</u>

♪ 4. <u>[coordinate how to] distribute weight properly</u>

♪ 5. <u>[make sure they] reset spinnaker if after a leeward rounding</u>

♪ 6. <u>make sure nothing is dragging in the water</u>

    7. <u>watch for hazards</u>

♪ keep an eye out for other boats or obstructions on the course and make sure collisions do not occur

♪ communicate with other boats as needed: starboard; tack or cross, come up, overlap, etc... it is best to count out loud after, "one-one thousand, two-one thousand, three-one thousand." this proves room and opportunity

♪ listen to calls from the bow about course changes needed for kelp, etc.

♪ 8. <u>[make sure you and they] prepare for windward set</u>. advise everyone on the boat of the plan prior to maneuvers, not just the skipper. remember to notify of any changes to previously made plans, especially last-minute ones

<u>Notice:</u> Check with your local governing bodies if there are any requirements to drive a boat. State of California requires a California Boater ID to drive a motor operated vessel.

Windward Set

General

Some Information in Chapter 3 <u>Racing Positions</u>

Team Procedures

1. coordinate in advance
2. prepare the spinnaker and pole
3. round the mark
4. stay out of the way of the tacking or gybing boom
5. hoist the spinnaker
6. close the hatch
7. drop the jib
8. trim the spinnaker
9. be prepared to assist round up or down
10. prepare for a gybe
11. make sure nothing is dragging in the water
12. distribute weight properly
13. watch for hazards

Bow

1. coordinate in advance

➤ communicate with the tactician if planning a standard or gybe set

➤ communicate with the tactician whether or not you have enough time to perform changing between a gybe set or standard set. you may have to leave it as is

2. prepare the spinnaker and pole

➤ I like to put the foot on the bottom and head on top so it is easy to see the spinnaker triangle having no wraps before and during the hoist when doing a hatch set

➤ make sure the foreguy is lead properly, not hanging up on the bow pulpit or headstay

➤ if you are changing the side of the set you can hook all sheets, afterguys and halyard together and pull around the headstay

➤ if you are changing the side of a hatch set you can just spin the spinnaker inside the hatch to the other side. sheets and afterguys to be reattached on proper side of headstay

➤ some people like to tape the sheets and/or halyard shackles closed

➢ some people tape the sheet and afterguy together a few feet back from being in the jaws of the pole

➢ sheets on top of everything. if you are doing a hatch set, sheets are likely to cross under the jib or jib sheets to attach

➢ sheets and afterguys attached separately to the spinnaker on both sides in case one comes loose off the spinnaker

➢ I put both sheets and afterguys in the jaws of the pole before the first set. no cowboy needed. you can temporarily use the sheet if the afterguy comes loose from the sail or pole because the sheet is already in the pole

➢ if topping lift is outside the jib sheets you can hook it up early and tape it to a stanchion near the spreaders, but not behind

➢ ensure halyard is hooked up

➢ I usually do a hatch set when I know what spinnaker is going to be used before the start. I hook up all the sheets, afterguys and the halyard ahead of time. I tape the halyard to a stanchion near the bow pulpit. then it is out of the way of the jib and ready to be hoisted

➢ make sure the spinnaker and pole are hooked up and clear to be raised. under the jib but not under lifelines or foreguy

➢ make sure there is slack in the foreguy so the pole can be raised

➢ make sure there is slack in the lazy jib sheet that is over the pole so the pole can be raised

➢ make sure the pole trip line is not snagged, causing it to trip

➢ a lot of time you can raise the topping lift while sitting on the rail. pull on the afterguy to keep the pole from hanging up on the headstay or bow pulpit. this can be done when on layline, or around 5 boat lengths to the mark

➢ if topping lift is outside the jib sheets and you have already broken the tape, the boat can still be tacked. just have pit leave it not cleated and the jib will usually not get hung up. make sure to re-tape the topping lift or manually hold it forward of the mast and spreaders during tacks

➢ if you can, have an alligator clip at the mast to hold the topping lift up in case the pit is busy

➢ raise the butt end of the pole to proper height and ensure that it is secured in place around 3 boat lengths to the mark. this usually requires being set in two sets of alligator clips

➢ if you are doing a hatch set, flip open the hatch and shout "hatch open" at about 2 boat lengths to the mark. make sure nothing is trapped underneath it

➢ call back to the boat "pre-feed" to get the spinnaker to the pole at about 1 boat length to the mark

➤ assist with pre-feeding while making sure the spinnaker does not fill with air or water. if pre-feeding with both sheets and afterguys in the jaws pre-feed both to make sure no loops are hanging in front of the jaws

➤ sometimes the boat approaches the mark on the opposite tack and will gybe around it. this is also known as 'button-hooking the mark.' the pole is trapped and thus cannot be raised 5 boat lengths prior to the mark. move the spinnaker up to the bow pulpit to have an early pre-feed. make sure not to let the sail fill with water or air. make sure the cockpit knows you are doing this so they can keep slack while upwind and pre-feed without your assistance directly after heading downwind

➤ if circumstances present where the pole will be trapped on layline, just trip the lines from the jaws of the pole. this can also be done if button-hooking the mark and the time required to raise the pole prior to hoist is predicted to be too long

➤ you can also trip the pole prior to hoist if you are planning to gybe immediately after the spinnaker set

➤ listen for instructions from the back of the boat that may delay the set of the spinnaker. they may also ask for a quick gybe after finishing the set and jib takedown

➤ ensure the spinnaker and halyard are in front of the spreaders before and during the hoist

➤ ensure the pole is topped and spinnaker is pre-fed prior to hoist

➤ I usually sit on the deck next to the spinnaker with my feet braced against something. I wrap my arms around the spinnaker head with only finger tips touching. keep your arms low to help keep the pre-fed spinnaker from filling. any major pressure on the sail will not injure you or pull you overboard, but just pull through your not-interlocked hands. this keeps the spinnaker from filling, going overboard, or hitting the mark while being raised. this can usually allow for some slow pre-hoisting of the spinnaker.

➤ 3. round the mark

➤ 4. stay out of the way of the tacking or gybing boom

    5. hoist the spinnaker

➤ assist the spinnaker out of the hatch or sail bag and keep from getting caught on: pulpit, lifelines, spreaders, people, etc.

➤ keep feet clear of sheets, afterguys, and spinnaker

➤ pull out one side of the spinnaker helping to keep it from getting wrapped while going up

➤ try to keep an eye out for any boats or obstructions

➤ look up and clear any twists or problems prior to the spinnaker filling with air

➢ assist the mast person with the hoist if needed

➢ when the spinnaker fills call out "you have a chute." that way the spinnaker trimmer knows they can ease the sheet if needed

➢ 6. close the hatch as soon as possible. always know where the hatch is on the boat to keep from falling into the hole

➢ 7. drop the jib when spinnaker is fully up, usually call "jib down" to notify pit you are ready. you can pull down on the luff. you can use open hands swiping at the sail pushing it downwards. grabbing can get fingers hurt

➢ ensure the jib does not go overboard

➢ if the sail is in a headfoil make sure the jib is in the pre-feeder and foil

➢ attach fraculator to the halyard shackle where the line attaches. this allows the jaws of the halyard shackle to open to change headsails without de-fraculating

10. prepare for a gybe

➢ clear the spinnaker sheet to prepare for gybe

➢ if doing dip pole: prepare for a gybe by having approximately 3 arm lengths of lazy afterguy prior to cockpit wrapping the winch

➢ push or roll the jib forward to get the deck clear of sail

➢ put a sail tie or bungie over the jib if needed to hold it on deck. make sure to not trap anything that will be needed later: sheets, guys, etc.

➢ stepping on any sail under way is highly likely to slip along the surface of the deck and take you with it

➢ 11. make sure nothing is dragging in the water

12. distribute weight properly

➢ if mast person is assisting, notify them when they are no longer needed

➢ everyone stay off the bow as much as possible

➢ sit down in the proper place for weight distribution. standing up blocks the skipper's view and creates wind drag

➢ 13. watch for hazards. keep an eye out for hazards on and in the water

Mast

1. coordinate in advance   &

2. prepare the spinnaker and pole

○ with bow telling you the order of the sequence and who does what stay on the rail as long as possible

○ know which halyard you will be jumping and get to the spinnaker halyard about 1 boat length from the mark

○ keep feet clear of sheets, afterguys, and spinnaker. know that the closer to the mast your feet are with no lines between is the safest

○ assist with topping lift and/or butt end of the pole to get the pole in the proper position

○ work with bow to possibly sneak the spinnaker halyard up

○ 3. round the mark

○ 4. stay out of the way of the tacking or gybing boom

    5. hoist the spinnaker

○ wait for the tactician to call "hoist," and then jump the halyard as fast as you can

○ make sure that the spinnaker is not caught up on anything, including the spreaders. stop hoist until it is clear. ask for bow assistance to get it clear if needed

○ hoist with hand over hand as fast as possible until you cannot anymore. then slide your hands up and down the halyard without letting go of the halyard. a second person can assist if both are doing this. when there is a lot of resistance, I just grab on and buckle my knees. this allows my body weight to pull the sail up like I lifted my feet and hung on the halyard

○ avoid pulling the halyard out away from the mast because pit is not as able to retrieve all the slack

○ make sure pit is keeping up so you are not holding the spinnaker by yourself. it will burn through your hands

○ loops can form and block the halyard if there is too much halyard on the deck. make sure pit is keeping up with retrieving the slack at the same time. if a loop stops the halyard from going through the block, tug hard on the loose halyard on the deck until the loop comes out

○ if you can, have an alligator clip on the mast to hold the spinnaker halyard in case pit cannot keep up

○ ensure all the slack is out of the halyard and look up to make sure the spinnaker is all the way up. holler "made" if it is so

○ if the halyard is not up all the way prior to the sail filling, you may still be able to continue jumping the halyard. you may need assistance from a second person to jump it, or you may need the pit to grind it up

○ 6. close the hatch as soon as possible. always know where the hatch is on the boat to keep from falling into the hole

    7. drop the jib

○ assist with the takedown of the jib keeping it from going overboard until bow states you are no longer needed, then proceed off the bow

○ be understanding of where the boom is or where it may end up so you can keep from getting hit with it

○ stepping on any sail under way is highly likely to slip along the surface of the deck and take you with it

○ 12. <u>distribute [your] weight properly</u>. sit down. standing up blocks the skippers view and creates wind drag

○ 13. <u>watch for hazards</u>

Pit

1. <u>coordinate in advance</u>   &

2. <u>prepare the spinnaker and pole</u>

▪ if anybody is on deck forward of pit you are in charge of watching them and assisting with everything they may need. keep your eyes forward as much as possible. any amount of time looking down, looking at the cockpit, or looking elsewhere, means longer response time for things the person on the bow needs. more time before responses can mean more pulling or holding of something under load by the person on the bow; it always means more energy consumption just from standing on a usually tilted and bouncing bow. it is also a safety thing

▪ stay on the rail for as long as you can

▪ make sure jib halyard is still clear and ready to be dropped

▪ make sure there is slack in the foreguy and lazy jib sheet so the pole can be raised

▪ make sure the cam cleats are closed for spinnaker halyard and topping lift that is being raised prior to pulling

▪ make sure the spinnaker halyard is wrapped on a winch prior to rounding

▪ a lot of the time you can raise the topping lift while sitting on the rail. bow pulls on the afterguy to keep the pole from hanging up on the headstay or bow pulpit. this can be done when on layline, or around 5 boat lengths to the mark

▪ be prepared to drop the pole if you need to tack

▪ sometimes the boat approaches the mark on the opposite tack and will gybe around it. this is also known as 'button-hooking the mark.' the pole is trapped and thus cannot be raised 5 boat lengths prior to the mark. it is best to have someone else raise the pole while you raise the halyard

▪ if you cannot raise the pole until the last minute, you may ask for assistance from another person to do the topping lift

- 3. <u>round the mark</u>

- 4. <u>stay out of the way of the tacking or gybing boom</u>

  5. <u>hoist the spinnaker</u>

- when mast starts pulling, you pull the spinnaker halyard with 'big arms.' elbows are moving past the shoulders and then dropping the line on the floor at your feet. pull with strength so that mast is not taking all the weight up. keep tension on the halyard at all times! any movement by mast on the halyard is instantly pulled by pit to not have any slack on the halyard

- make sure that the spinnaker is not caught up on anything. stop hoist until clear

- if the halyard is not up all the way prior to the sail filling, be prepared for mast to continue jumping the halyard if they can. pull in the slack immediately. watch forward to make sure you do not need to hoist more with the mast person. the mast person should not have to hoist alone

- if jumping is not able to be done anymore, grind the halyard up with mast or bow telling you the distance until made

  7. <u>drop the jib</u>

- do this as soon as possible, with at least a wrap or two on the winch. keep your fingers clear. stop dropping the jib if it is going overboard and allow the bow to collect it. you can also use the cam cleat to do this

- take the halyard off the winch after the first half of the jib is down. feed line to the other side of the cam cleat if needed to help the sail drop quickly. less pulling required by the bowperson means more conserved energy. getting the jib out of the way allows the spinnaker to fill and allows the bowperson to get off the bow

- you may get a second person to assist with this.

  8. <u>trim the spinnaker</u>

- adjust the topping lift to ensure the pole is at the correct height. then snug the foreguy so that the pole does not bounce. you may get a second person to assist with the foreguy

- play the foreguy as the pole is moved fore and aft. you may get someone to assist with this. the person controlling the pole may be this person

- listen for calls that the tip of the pole may need to be raised or lowered. take the foreguy into account when adjusting topping lift

- listen and relay information to and from the front of the boat

- 9. <u>be prepared to assist round up or down</u>. hold the boom vang when in heavy wind and wait for the call to ease

- let off outhaul, boom vang, and cunningham as main trimmer desires. most boats do not have them near the main

- run your hand over the whole length of the spinnaker halyard and loosely drop it where you desire it to stay to make sure it is clear for the takedown

- 12. <u>distribute [your] weight properly</u>

Cockpit

1. <u>coordinate in advance</u> &

2. <u>prepare the spinnaker and pole</u>

◇ coordinate who does what

◇ always listen for people calling out for assistance needed

◇ always keep an eye forward when pulling or releasing something

◇ stay on the rail for as long as possible

◇ ensure the sheet and afterguy are slack enough for the tip of the pole to be raised

◇ unwrap the lazy jib sheet from the winch so that the butt end of the pole can be raised

◇ wrap the afterguy around the winch. only pull on it when bow mentions to "pre-feed." only pre-feed until the spinnaker is at the pole and the pole is barely off the headstay. if the sheet is in the jaws of the pole, pre-feed it at the same time to prevent loops from forming between the jaws and the spinnaker clew

◇ sometimes the boat approaches the mark on the opposite tack and will gybe around it. this is also known as 'button-hooking the mark.' the pole is trapped and thus cannot be raised 5 boat lengths prior to the mark. the bow should have set the spinnaker near the bow pulpit so you can pre-feed as the spinnaker is being hoisted. keep slack until sailing downwind to make sure the sail does not fill with water or air

◇ do not allow the jib to go out too much, even if replacing the jib sheet with the spinnaker sheet on the winch. either an alligator cleat or a 'hobbler' can be used to do this

◇ assist pit if needed

◇ 3. <u>round the mark</u>

◇ 4. <u>stay out of the way of the tacking or gybing boom</u>

◇ pull the sheet back to at least the cockpit when "hoist" is called. this helps keep the spinnaker from wrapping (5. <u>[assist with hoisting] the spinnaker</u>)

8. trim the spinnaker

◇ always make sure that the pole is not resting on the headstay

◇ the pole usually ends up 90 degrees to the wind and in line with the boom

◇ the height of the pole is determined by matching the height of the clew

◇ wait until "made" is called by the mast person, meaning the spinnaker is all the way up. then, pull back on the afterguy until it is in position in line with the boom

◇ pulling the pole back will likely cause the sail to come out from behind the jib and fill with air. when the spinnaker is full, ease the sheet to proper sail trim

◇ clear the jib sheet after the jib is on the deck so that bow can move the sail forward

◇ communicate with the skipper about wind conditions

◇ the spinnaker can be flown without the pole. allow the spinnaker to fly a few feet in front of the headstay by keeping the sheets and afterguys loose enough. this is called 'free-flying' the spinnaker. that way if the boat rolls, the spinnaker is able to shift freely to stay full of wind. if the spinnaker starts to shift violently pull the spinnaker in tight to the headstay. this is also known as 'strapping' the spinnaker

◇ strap the foot of the spinnaker prior to waves

◇ do not let the windward clew pass onto the leeward side of the headstay. it could get caught and pull on the pin releasing the afterguy or sheet from the spinnaker

◇ even if on a reach, always have some tension on the afterguy so that the headstay is not holding the pole

◇ trim the spinnaker to barely fold the edge on a slow and somewhat regular basis. slowly sheet in if the sail is folding too much. slowly ease out when it is not folding at all. you are usually playing the sheet back and forth unless the wind is super heavy in a constant direction. be careful not to play it too much or the wind will not be pulling the boat

◇ have a grinder ready to assist with sheeting in the spinnaker when the trimmer calls for it. usually "grind" is called. in order to not wear out a grinder you might say "okay" when grinding is no longer needed

◇ if the wind shifts forward and the sheet is not fast enough, let the pole forward also until the sail fills

◇ if the wind dies most people have a tendency to sheet in on the spinnaker sheet too much because the spinnaker collapses. be wary of this. if the wind does die, be cautious not to allow the spinnaker to wrap around the headstay or go through the wrong way and fill inside the headstay

◊ be watchful of the spinnaker getting caught on anything while flying. jib hanks are the usual suspect

◊ 9. be prepared to assist round up or down. ease the sheet quickly until the spinnaker is no longer full

◊ 10. prepare for a gybe

◊ 11. make sure nothing is dragging in the water

◊ 12. distribute [your] weight properly

Main Trim

1. coordinate in advance

❖ coordinate with the skipper and tactician when to ease the main way out

❖ make sure outhaul, cunningham, and boom vang are set properly

❖ 3. round the mark

❖ make sure everyone 4. stay[s] out of the way of the tacking or gybing boom and main sheet

❖ in heavy wind, make sure someone is holding onto the boom vang to ease it to help prevent round ups (9. [make sure you and another are] prepared to assist round up or down)

❖ watch forward for any obstacles because the bowperson is busy: boats, kelp, obstructions, etc. (13. watch for hazards)

❖ watch forward to call out if there are any issues with the set

Skipper

☐ keep a little distance from the mark so that the spinnaker does not touch (3. round the mark)

☐ 4. stay out of the way of the tacking or gybing boom

5. hoist the spinnaker

☐ turn down when the halyard is not straight up from the head of the spinnaker. it gets blown back into the rigging when too hard on the wind

☐ turn down when you see the chute, the lines, or people flopping all over the place. when people cannot stand up well, they cannot do their task well

☐ if the boat gets out of control in heavy wind call to ease the boom vang (9. be prepared to [ask for assistance prior to] round up or down)

☐ 13. watch for hazards [ahead only]

Tactician

1. coordinate in advance

♪ coordinate with bow in advance that the correct spinnaker is hooked up and ready to hoist

♪ adjust layline for slide due to high wind and/or current

♪ adjust layline for slide due to being in the bad air of other boats in front of or above you

♪ try to do a bear away set for consistency

♪ advise in advance if needing to delay the spinnaker hoist

♪ advise in advance if deciding to gybe quickly after the set

♪ call out to other boats if they are in need to know the rules based on your position (13. [part of] watch for hazards)

♪ 2. [make sure they] prepare the spinnaker and pole. try to give time to get the spinnaker preparation done prior to the rounding and set

♪ 3. round the mark

♪ 4. stay out of the way of the tacking or gybing boom

5. hoist the spinnaker

♪ call a cadence sequence to perform the tasks during the set

♪ make sure heads are out of the way of the boom during tack or gybe

♪ 6. [make sure they] close the hatch

♪ 7. [make sure they] drop the jib

♪ 8. [make sure they] trim the spinnaker

♪ 9. [make sure they are] prepared to assist round up or down

♪ 10. [make sure they] prepare for a gybe

♪ 11. make sure nothing is dragging in the water

♪ 12. [coordinate how to] distribute weight properly

♪ 13. watch for hazards

Set

Port of Long Beach with downtown Long Beach, Queen Mary, Carnival Cruise ship, and the cruise ship terminal that is the dome that was the home of the Spruce Goose. The Spruce Goose is the largest wooden plane every constructed. Little known fact, the Spruce Goose was made out of birch and should have been called the 'Birch Bird.' Taken while on a birthday helicopter ride during the Long Beach Festival of Flight 2019.

U.S.S. Iowa Battleship & Vincent Thomas Bridge

For information the S.S. Lane Victory is also a ship to see

Gybe (End for End)

General

Some Information in Chapter 3 <u>Racing Positions</u>

Team Procedures

1. coordinate in advance
2. prepare the lines and pole
3. square the pole back
4. trip the pole and free fly the spinnaker
5. stay out of the way of the gybing boom
6. set the pole
7. trim the spinnaker
8. be prepared to assist round up or down
9. prepare for another gybe (if needed)
10. prepare for spinnaker takedown (if next)
11. make sure nothing is dragging in the water
12. distribute weight properly
13. watch for hazards

Bow

➢ 1. <u>coordinate in advance</u> with mast the order of the sequence and who does what. how your trip lines on the pole are run will determine who trips what end of the pole

　　2. prepare the lines and pole

➢ make sure the pole is lowered to a predetermined height

➢ stand with the jib sheet over your shoulder on the side of the soon to be new afterguy

➢ hold the soon to be new afterguy in your hand in preparation for putting it in the jaws of the pole. be as close to the clew of the spinnaker as possible; **cinch up when you can**. always use the left hand on the port side of the boat and the right hand on the starboard side. always do palm up or palm down the same way every time. keep your thumb pointing out in the same direction every time, so that you know which way the spinnaker is in comparison to your thumb direction. do not let go of your hand hold so you know the location of the clew

➢ make sure the skipper turns down to 3. <u>square the pole back</u> prior to trip if previously on a reach

➢ (mast or bow) trip the inboard end of pole off the mast when you hear "trip" from the back of the boat, or when the boat begins to turn. leave the outboard end on as long as possible to help with control of the spinnaker (4. trip the pole and [cockpit free flys] the spinnaker)

➢ grab the free end of the pole and feed it under the jib sheet. assist mast with controlling the spinnaker and pole to keep it from moving around too much

➢ (mast or bow) trip the outboard end of the pole

➢ 5. stay out of the way of the gybing boom

6. set the pole

➢ insert the afterguy into the jaws of the pole with the spinnaker clew side forward. your thumb direction will help you with that. I prefer palm up with thumb facing aft, so I draw the hand forward past the jaws and drop the line into the jaws. the line is usually more taught going aft for the line to set the jaws closed. cinch up to the clew clearing any loops in the line. insert the line and make sure the jaws set

➢ sometimes in heavy wind if the spinnaker is very far forward of the headstay, tripping the outboard end can be done after the line is in the jaws on the windward side

➢ ensure there are no loops in the afterguy, especially not around the end of the pole

➢ push the tip of the pole forward to the clew and outboard

➢ assist mast with attaching the inboard end of the pole if needed

➢ pull the afterguy back with the trimmer if a lot of distance is needed to be pulled in (7. [assist cockpit with trimming] the spinnaker)

9. prepare for another gybe (if needed)   &

10. prepare for spinnaker takedown (if next)

➢ asses all lines to ensure gybe went properly and did not trap anything

➢ ensure that if you have a separate sheet from the guy (not standard) it is above the pole, then cowboy it by throwing a loop and letting it wrap around the afterguy

➢ 11. make sure nothing is dragging in the water

➢ sit down and 12. distribute [your] weight properly

➢ 13. watch for hazards

Mast

O 1. coordinate in advance with bow telling you the order of the sequence and who does what. how your trip lines on the pole are run will determine who trips what end of the pole

○ lower the butt end of the pole to a predetermined height (2. prepare the lines and pole)

○ make sure the skipper turns down to 3. square the pole back prior to trip if previously on a reach

4. trip the pole and [cockpit free flys] the spinnaker

○ (mast or bow) trip the butt end of pole off the mast when you hear "trip" from the back of the boat, or when the boat begins to turn. leave the outboard end on as long as possible to help with control of the spinnaker

○ control the pole from moving around too much, which will in turn control the spinnaker

○ (mast or bow) trip the outboard end of the pole

○ sometimes in heavy wind if the spinnaker is way far forward of the headstay, tripping the outboard end can be done after the line is in the jaws on the windward side

○ 5. stay out of the way of the gybing boom

6. set the pole

○ strip the other jib sheet off the pole. attach the butt end of the pole to the mast and call "made"

○ if you are having trouble attaching the butt end of the pole ask the skipper to turn down

○ sit down and 12. distribute [your] weight properly

○ 13. watch for hazards

Pit

▪ if anybody is on deck forward of pit you are in charge of watching them and assisting with everything they may need. keep your eyes forward as much as possible. any amount of time looking down, looking at the cockpit, or looking elsewhere, means longer response time for things the person on the bow needs. more time before responses can mean more pulling or holding of something under load by the person on the bow; it always means more energy consumption just from standing on a usually tilted and bouncing bow. it is also a safety thing

1. coordinate in advance

▪ work with the bow on whether to release the foreguy so the pole can be moved into place, or keep tension on it so that the pole can be controlled a little more easily. keeping tension on the foreguy allows bow team to hold onto the pole in choppy waters to steady themselves. keeping tension means to have a hand on the line or to have one wrap on a winch, but ease as needed

- always relay info back and forth across the boat

- lower the topping lift to a predetermined height (2. prepare the lines and pole)

- make sure the skipper turns down to 3. square the pole back prior to trip if previously on a reach

- 5. stay out of the way of the gybing boom

    6. set the pole

- raise topping lift back up to sailing height after "made"

- snug foreguy

- play the foreguy as the pole is moved fore and aft. you may get someone to assist with this. the person controlling the pole may be this person

- hold the boom vang when in heavy wind and wait for the call to ease (8. be prepared to assist round up or down)

- 12. distribute [your] weight properly

Cockpit

◇ 1. coordinate in advance who does what

◇ always listen for people calling out for assistance needed

◇ always keep an eye forward when pulling or releasing something

◇ make sure the skipper turns down to 3. square the pole back prior to trip if previously on a reach

    4. [bow trips] the pole and [you] free fly the spinnaker

◇ fly the spinnaker completely full through the gybe

◇ free-fly the spinnaker. this allows the boat to turn inside the spinnaker while it flies full (some pulling needed). this also allows the spinnaker some latitude to shift a little without causing the boat to crash

◇ free-flying can also be done if you are hoisting or flying the spinnaker without a pole

◇ you should practice at least one or two gybes holding both sheets and controlling the spinnaker, keeping it full

◇ try to rotate the spinnaker completely to the other side of the headstay prior to the main gybing over

◇ 5. stay out of the way of the gybing boom

6. set the pole   &

7. trim the spinnaker

◇ do not adjust the spinnaker to help with mast attaching the butt end of the pole, the skipper should turn the boat down

◇ do not pull on the afterguy until you hear "made," then pull it into position

◇ ease the sheet accordingly when the afterguy is being set into place to keep the spinnaker full

◇ always watch the spinnaker and trim accordingly to keep it full

◇ 8. be prepared to assist round up or down. ease the sheet quickly until the spinnaker is no longer full

◇ 9. prepare for another gybe (if needed)

◇ 10. prepare for spinnaker takedown (if next)

◇ 11. make sure nothing is dragging in the water

◇ 12. distribute [your] weight properly

Main Trim

❖ make sure everyone 5. stay[s] out of the way of the gybing boom and main sheet

❖ if you are grinding the main in - do so until the boom is just about centered, then ease a lot out quickly to downwind trim

❖ if you are not grinding the main in - gather the main sheet and assist it across, making sure it is not hung up on anything. be sure you do not hold onto it or it will pull you overboard

❖ watch forward for any obstacles because the bowperson is busy: boats, kelp, obstructions, etc. (13. watch for hazards)

❖ watch forward to call out if there are any issues with the gybe

❖ in heavy wind, make sure someone is holding on to the boom vang to ease it to help prevent round ups (8. [make sure you and another are] prepared to assist round up or down)

Skipper

☐ turn down to 3. square the pole back prior to trip if previously on a reach

☐ 5. stay out of the way of the gybing boom

□ smooth turn and come out a little higher than normal to fill the spinnaker

□ turn the boat down if the bow team needs help to 6. set the pole attaching the butt end of the pole to the mast

□ if the boat gets out of control in heavy wind, call to ease the boom vang (10. be prepared to [ask for assistance prior to] round up or down)

□ 13. watch for hazards [ahead only]

Tactician

♪ 1. [make sure they] coordinate in advance

♪ 2. [make sure they] prepare the lines and pole

♪ make sure skipper turns down to 3. square the pole back prior to trip if previously on a reach

♪ call out a cadence during the gybe: prepare to gybe, square the pole, trip (as the boat starts to turn), ease the sheet, etc.

♪ notify everyone of "prepare to gybe"

♪ 4. [call out "trip" to] trip the pole and free fly the spinnaker

♪ 5. [make sure they] stay out of the way of the gybing boom

♪ make sure skipper turns the boat down if the bow team needs help to 6. set the pole attaching the butt end of the pole to the mast

♪ 7. [make sure they] trim the spinnaker

♪ 8. [make sure they are] prepared to assist round up or down

♪ 9. [make sure they] prepare for another gybe (if needed)

♪ 10. [make sure they] prepare for spinnaker takedown (if next)

♪ 11. make sure nothing is dragging in the water

♪ 12. [coordinate how to] distribute weight properly

♪ 13. watch for hazards

Pro Tip #1

Be extra vigilant to not get the spinnaker to backfill on the wrong side of the boat. This will cause the spinnaker to get pushed through the triangle between the headstay and the mast. Trimmers and skippers need to regulate turn rate and rotation of the spinnaker. If this happens, skipper turns back, while trimmers and bow help the spinnaker around the headstay.

Gybe (Dip Pole)

General

Some Information in Chapter 3 <u>Racing Positions</u>

Team Procedures

1. coordinate in advance
2. prepare the lines and pole
3. square the pole back
4. trip the pole and free fly the spinnaker
5. stay out of the way of the gybing boom
6. set the pole
7. trim the spinnaker
8. be prepared to assist round up or down
9. prepare for another gybe (if needed)
10. prepare for spinnaker takedown (if next)
11. make sure nothing is dragging in the water
12. distribute weight properly
13. watch for hazards

Bow

➢ 1. <u>coordinate in advance</u> with mast the order of the sequence and who does what

    2. prepare the lines and pole

➢ make sure the soon to be new sheet is not below the pole or it will hinder the gybe

➢ before a set I put the sheet in the jaws with the afterguy to help keep the sheet from dipping below the pole, make sure to prefeed both

➢ mast raises the butt end of the pole to a preset height when hearing "prepare to gybe"

➢ stand on the bow facing either the pole or forward. keep your head on the opposite side of the forestay so you will not get hit in the head with the pole

➢ hold the soon to be new afterguy in your hand in preparation for putting it in the jaws of the pole. be as close to the clew of the spinnaker as possible; **cinch up when you can**. always use the left hand on the port side of the boat and the right hand on the starboard side. always do palm up or palm down the same way every time. keep your thumb pointing out in the same direction every time, so that you know which

Dip

way the spinnaker is in comparison to your thumb direction. do not let go of your hand hold so you know the location of the clew

➤ make sure the skipper turns down to 3. square the pole back prior to trip if previously on a reach

4. trip the pole and [cockpit free flys] the spinnaker

➤ bow usually trips the pole because the trip line can then be used to pull the pole forward. but sometimes mast is looking for something to do and wants to trip

➤ if mast is tripping the pole you can use the foreguy to pull the pole toward you if needed

➤ grab the pole with your free hand and pull it up on your shoulder. simultaneously move over to allow the pole to cross to the other side of the forestay

➤ make sure that the trip line is not held down after you grab the pole

➤ move the pole over your head, usually while ducking. turn facing the direction the pole will end up on

➤ 5. stay out of the way of the gybing boom

6. set the pole

➤ guide the pole to your hand with the afterguy

➤ cinch up to the clew clearing any loops in the line. insert the afterguy into the jaws of the pole with the spinnaker clew side forward. your thumb direction will help you with that. I prefer palm up with thumb facing aft, so I draw the hand forward past the jaws and drop the line into the jaws. the line is usually more taught going aft for the line to set the jaws closed. insert the line and make sure the jaws set

➤ ensure there are no loops in the afterguy, especially not around the end of the pole

➤ ensure the spinnaker is rotated completely around the headstay and call "made." raising the pole prior to the spinnaker being fully rotated can cause the pole to stab and puncture the sail. if the spinnaker is collapsed, you can pull the sheet yourself to rotate the spinnaker (7. [part of assisting cockpit with trimming] the spinnaker)

➤ after you call "made," push the pole up and forward, then grab the afterguy and run backwards to help the trimmer get the clew to the pole (7. [assist cockpit with trimming] the spinnaker)

9. prepare for another gybe (if needed)   &

10. prepare for spinnaker takedown (if next)

➤ prepare for the next gybe by having approximately 3 arm lengths of lazy afterguy prior to the cockpit wrapping the winch

➢ ensure that the sheet is above the pole, then 'cowboy' it by throwing a loop and letting it wrap around the afterguy

➢ asses all lines to ensure gybe went properly and did not trap anything

➢ 11. <u>make sure nothing is dragging in the water</u>

➢ sit down and 12. <u>distribute [your] weight properly</u>

➢ 13. <u>watch for hazards</u>

Mast

○ 1. <u>coordinate in advance</u> with bow telling you the order of the sequence and who does what

○ raise the butt end of the pole to a preset height when hearing "prepare to gybe" (2. <u>prepare the lines and pole</u>)

○ make sure the skipper turns down to 3. <u>square the pole back</u> prior to trip if previously on a reach

    4. <u>trip the pole and [cockpit free flys] the spinnaker</u>

○ bow usually trips the pole because the trip line can then be used to pull the pole forward. but sometimes mast is looking for something to do and wants to trip

○ make sure that the trip line is not held down after bow grabs the pole

○ 5. <u>stay out of the way of the gybing boom</u>

○ after "made" is called, put the butt end of the pole back to sailing position (6. <u>set the pole</u>)

○ make sure bow "cowboys" the sheet around the afterguy; throws a loop that twists around the taught line to keep it from dipping below the pole

○ pass the lazy afterguy to bow to get their slack for the next gybe

○ sit down and 12. <u>distribute [your] weight properly</u>

○ 13. <u>watch for hazards</u>

Pit

▪ if anybody is on deck forward of pit you are in charge of watching them and assisting with everything they may need. keep your eyes forward as much as possible. any amount of time looking down, looking at the cockpit, or looking elsewhere, means longer response time for things the person on the bow needs. more time before responses can mean more pulling or holding of something under load by the person on the bow; it always means more energy consumption just from standing on a usually tilted and bouncing bow. it is also a safety thing

▪ always relay info back and forth across the boat (1. <u>coordinate in advance</u>)

▪ make sure the skipper turns down to 3. <u>square the pole back</u> prior to trip if previously on a reach

<u>4. trip the pole and [cockpit free flys] the spinnaker</u>

▪ drop the topping lift quickly a couple feet when you see bow pull on the trip line. usually tactician has called "trip." this gets the pole to drop clear of the old afterguy as the jaws open

▪ dropping the topping lift too much could drop the pole on the lifelines, in the water, or on bow's head

▪ wait until the pole starts swinging toward the bowperson

▪ drop the topping lift to below shoulder level of the bowperson. this ensures that if the pole swings fast bow will not get hit in the head

▪ wait until bow has the pole and let go of the topping lift completely

▪ 5. <u>stay out of the way of the gybing boom</u>

<u>6. set the pole</u>

▪ haul the topping lift up into sailing position after hearing "made"

▪ snug foreguy

▪ play the foreguy as the pole is moved fore and aft. you may get someone to assist with this. the person controlling the pole may be this person

▪ hold the boom vang when in heavy wind and wait for the call to ease (8. <u>be prepared to assist round up or down</u>)

▪ 12. <u>distribute [your] weight properly</u>

Cockpit

◇ 1. <u>coordinate in advance</u> who does what

◇ always listen for people calling out for assistance needed

◇ always keep an eye forward when pulling or releasing something

◇ make sure the bow has enough length in the lazy guy then wrap the winch and put the handle in (2. <u>prepare the lines and pole</u>)

◇ make sure the skipper turns down to 3. <u>square the pole back</u> prior to trip if previously on a reach

◇ always listen for people calling out for assistance needed

4. [bow trips] the pole and [you] free fly the spinnaker

◇ fly the spinnaker completely full through the gybe

◇ free-fly the spinnaker. this allows the boat to turn inside the spinnaker while it flies full (some pulling needed). this also allows the spinnaker some latitude to shift a little without causing the boat to crash

◇ free-flying can also be done if you are hoisting or flying the spinnaker without a pole

◇ you should practice at least one or two gybes holding both sheets and controlling the spinnaker, keeping it full

◇ try to rotate the spinnaker completely to the other side of the headstay prior to the main gybing over

◇ make sure bow has their slack in the afterguy that will be used on the next gybe prior to wrapping the winch

◇ 5. stay out of the way of the gybing boom

6. set the pole &

7. trim the spinnaker

◇ do not pull on the afterguy until you hear "made," then pull it into position

◇ ease the sheet accordingly when the afterguy is being set into place to keep the spinnaker full

◇ transfer the load from the sheet to the afterguy once the afterguy has been snugged to the end of the pole

◇ always watch the spinnaker and trim accordingly to keep it full

◇ keep some tension on the old sheet until bow "cowboys" to keep it from dipping below the pole tip

◇ 8. be prepared to assist round up or down. ease the sheet quickly until the spinnaker is no longer full

◇ 9. prepare for another gybe (if needed)

◇ 10. prepare for spinnaker takedown (if next)

◇ 11. make sure nothing is dragging in the water

◇ 12. distribute [your] weight properly

Main Trim

❖ make sure everyone 5. stay[s] out of the way of the gybing boom and main sheet

❖ if you are grinding the main in - do so until the boom is just about centered, then ease a lot out quickly to downwind trim

❖ if you are not grinding the main in - gather the main sheet and assist it across, making sure it is not hung up on anything. be sure you do not hold onto it or it will pull you overboard

❖ watch forward for any obstacles because the bowperson is busy: boats, kelp, obstructions, etc. (13. watch for hazards)

❖ watch forward to call out if there are any issues with the gybe

❖ in heavy wind, make sure someone is holding on to the boom vang to ease it to help prevent round ups (8. [make sure you and another are] prepared to assist round up or down)

Skipper

☐ turn down to 3. square the pole back prior to trip if previously on a reach

☐ smooth turn and come out a little higher than normal to fill the spinnaker

☐ 5. stay out of the way of the gybing boom

☐ turn the boat down if the bow team needs help making the jaws

☐ if the boat gets out of control in heavy wind, call to ease the boom vang (10. be prepared to [ask for assistance prior to] round up or down)

☐ 13. watch for hazards [ahead only]

Tactician

♪ 1. [make sure they] coordinate in advance

♪ 2. [make sure they] prepare the lines and pole

♪ make sure skipper turns down to 3. square the pole back prior to trip if previously on a reach

♪ call out a cadence during the gybe: prepare to gybe, square the pole, trip (as the boat starts to turn), ease the sheet, etc.

♪ notify everyone of "prepare to gybe"

♪ 4. [call out "trip" to] trip the pole and free fly the spinnaker

♪ 5. [make sure they] stay out of the way of the gybing boom

♪ make sure skipper turns the boat down if the bow team needs help to 6. set the pole attaching the butt end of the pole to the mast

♪ 7. [make sure they] trim the spinnaker
♪ 8. [make sure they are] prepared to assist round up or down
♪ 9. [make sure they] prepare for another gybe (if needed)
♪ 10. [make sure they] prepare for spinnaker takedown (if next)
♪ 11. make sure nothing is dragging in the water
♪ 12. [coordinate how to] distribute weight properly
♪ 13. watch for hazards

Pro Tip #2

If you get a twist or "wrap" in the spinnaker the ease of freeing it depends on how tight it is. Spin trimmer can try sheeting in a lot which may pull it open. Mast or someone free can assist by pulling back and down on the sheet or the rear spinnaker tape. Bow can assist by pulling forward and down on the forward spinnaker tape. Sometimes dropping the jib and letting it fill with air can help it pop open. Twists in the body or head of the spinnaker will unfurl upwards. Twists in the tack or clew will unfurl outwards, pull on the foot tape if you can. Sometimes you have to drop the halyard 5 or 6 feet. Other times you have to drop the spinnaker completely to unravel it on the deck and rehoist. When rehoisting get a couple people on the jumping and on tailing to hopefully get the spinnaker back up before filling.

Huntington Beach Air Show with the Blue Angels from my father's boat

Leeward Rounding

Types of Leeward Roundings

Port Gybe - Port Side to - Port Side Takedown

Port Gybe - Starboard Side to - Port Side Takedown

Starboard Gybe - Port Side to - Port Side Takedown

Starboard Gybe - Starboard Side to - Port Side Takedown

Port Gybe - Port Side to - Starboard Side Takedown

Port Gybe - Starboard Side to - Starboard Side Takedown

Starboard Gybe - Port Side to - Starboard Side Takedown

Starboard Gybe - Starboard Side to - Starboard Side Takedown

General

The leeward rounding is the hardest maneuver to perform going around the course. Most of the issues with leeward roundings are because there has not been enough time for the bow team to perform the work prior to the rounding. Leeward roundings need more time in general than just a spinnaker takedown after finishing. Heavy winds and/or heavy seas require more time allotment for takedown. Often the skipper or tactician is screaming bloody murder for the halyard to be dropped. Screaming or rapidly repeating something does not get the task done well.

The skipper should be focused on driving properly for the maneuvers. The tactician should be doing the following: reminding bow to make sure the jib is not trapped; coordinating the procedures with bow; allowing the proper time for the takedown; advising the skipper of the direction of travel to assist the takedown even if it requires sailing more downwind when past the mark; advising the skipper of any direction changes required for boats in the area; calling the cadence of the maneuver calmly; and watching the maneuver and calling out calmly but loudly any issues that need to be fixed. Pit also calls out any issues that need to be fixed. If an issue is not too bad or can be fixed after the main part of the maneuver, it would be best to wait.

Often the bow and mast people are so up close and personal with everything going on they cannot see some issues; being notified helps them jump into action to fix it. If an issue is going to impede the progress of the maneuver, speaking up is key. In a couple words state the issue (or fix), then pause. Typically, with all the preoccupation of a set of goals, along with the sounds of the wind, waves, and sails, a repeat of the issue is needed. If the team is quiet during the maneuver, the first call out gets everyone's attention that there is something that needs fixing: as it should. The second callout is when everyone is paying attention and they hear exactly what the issue is. The responsible person(s) should respond with a verbal reply or action toward fixing the issue. If that is not working, call out their name, make sure they respond, and tell them.

Decent communication is key, and not just clarity of purpose. Everyone is out to have fun, so do your best to communicate in a way that will not upset others. Above is the way to get people's attention without causing tension. Two more steps happen that need to be considered: reply by the person needing to perform the action, and the continued actions of the initial caller/person requesting said action. A thumbs up, fist symbolizing hold, or any physical response works only if the person is looking at you. Some good verbal responses are as follows: copy; 10-4; affirmative; on it, etc. If you are replying a negative answer, further explanation of another option is usually needed. Negative replies are as follows: hold; 1 second; not able to, etc. If help is needed by someone else, the reply could also be "(insert action) please." The key is for communication to be short, precise, even toned, and impersonal. This keeps someone from becoming offended. Any reply should be heard by everyone, since enough pause by the initial caller would allow for it. The initial caller shall further pause and reflect upon the reply answer prior to proceeding. An understanding that some items cannot be performed instantly is needed. You are not in their position, so let them do their part to assist the team. The details and/or positions can be swapped after the race if needed. When someone on the team is not able to perform the task instantly, it is usually because another task is more important at the time.

Dropping the halyard prior to the bow being ready for it is a recipe for disaster. Any little thing can cause the spinnaker to not come down right, dropping into the water, filling with air upwind, or coming down trapping the jib from moving. Preparation is not that difficult: stowing the pole without trapping anything, raising the jib, and opening the hatch without trapping anything. After those things the pit person needs to listen and follow the bow and mast people solely. It is a requirement for the foot to be on the deck or in the hatch and the clews to be gathered and pulled tightly. The spinnaker halyard in most cases can be completely blown and run down really quickly after the chute is collapsed. The goal is to have the spinnaker down prior to even starting to turn the mark and heading up into the wind. I know it is not preferable, but I have held the spinnaker in my arms pulling down hard to keep the 'tapes' taught and the boat went upwind. The pit kept a lot of tension on while mast (and/or squirrel) pulled the spinnaker down. I must reiterate, the main point of a spinnaker takedown is working together to get the spinnaker collapsed prior to the halyard being released.

Pro Tip #3

If you have a boat with the main sheet coming out of the mast: Mast can usually get free to help jump the main sheet while rounding the mark. The spinnaker should be down and under control prior to turning up. This saves time of the main trimmer grinding in all the slack. Make sure the main trimmer knows this is happening and is tailing.

Running down the outside of the Long Beach breakwater. In the background are: downtown L.B, Carnival cruise ship and dome terminal, L.B. convention center Wyland painted whale wall

Leeward

Why Sailboat Racing Is So Difficult & Fun

<u>Choose the correct action</u>

(first you must correctly assess the situation, then also know what others will be doing)

Get this and more free resources to share and use at my website www.TeamCoordinatedRacing.com

The three points to performing an action / maneuver during sailboat racing

<u>Perform the correct degree of action</u>

(too little or too much action has consequences)

All 6-12 people are trying to coordinate the three above points with the others on the boat for every action they do

<u>Perform at the correct time</u>

(too soon or too late has consequences)

Spinnaker Takedown

General

Some Information in Chapter 3 <u>Racing Positions</u>

See Chapter 9 <u>Leeward Rounding</u> first

Team Procedures

1. coordinate in advance
2. prepare for the spinnaker takedown
3. raise the jib
4. square the pole back
5. remove and store the pole
6. depower, collapse, and takedown the spinnaker
7. get the spinnaker in the hatch (not catching wind)
8. stay out of the way of the tacking or gybing boom
9. round the mark
10. grind the jib into position
11. prepare for tack
12. distribute weight properly
13. reset for another spinnaker set
14. make sure nothing is dragging in the water
15. watch for hazards

Bow

<u>1. coordinate in advance</u>

➢ ask tactician which mark you will be rounding

➢ communicate with the boat and then mast to make sure everyone knows exactly what the procedure will be, which is usually: "jib up, pole down, spinnaker down on (port/starboard) side"

➢ avoid using terms to describe the takedown "standard takedown" or "mexican takedown" (sorry, this is a term used). terms require people to visualize what is happening on their own

➢ talk to squirrel to make sure they what to do

<u>2. prepare for the spinnaker takedown</u>

➢ make sure the jib is not trapped as early as possible prior to raising it. move it to the other side if needed

➢ unhook the foreguy to allow the jib to be raised on either gybe if you are doing end for end pole and the leeward buoy being rounded has not been determined. this will keep the jib from being trapped no matter how many more gybes are made. you may be able to hold the pole down yourself. a human guy may help. 'tweakers' may work to hold the spinnaker down. cockpit may have to strap the spinnaker

➤ if gybing close to the mark consider doing a poleless gybe. do not hook up or raise the pole during the gybe. stow the pole early. notify pit and cockpit you are doing this

➤ make sure squirrel gets into position

➤ 3. <u>raise the jib</u>. when the jib is being raised, make sure the spinnaker sheets are not caught and are being raised also

➤ make sure the skipper turns down to 4. <u>square the pole back</u> prior to trip if previously on a reach **

    5. <u>remove and store the pole</u>

➤ make sure to stow the pole early in a place that is out of the way for the rounding. it is best if you can get it into its normal upwind position. especially do this early in heavy breeze because the spinnaker takedown may take longer

➤ the butt end of the pole will need to be off the deck slightly to allow the spinnaker to go under and into the hatch

➤ make sure the topping lift will not hang up: pull slack into it, disconnect it, stow it, etc.

➤ make sure someone does human guy on the sheet

➤ open the hatch. call "hatch open." ensure that the jib sheets are not under it. always know where the hatch is on the boat to keep from falling into the hole

➤ if you have sheets and afterguys, you can grab the afterguy on the side of the takedown. lead it under the jib and spinnaker pole. either hand it to mast or down the hatch to the squirrel to pull on during the takedown

➤ inform cockpit to only take the takedown side spinnaker clew back to the pit area. too lose does not allow you to grab or hold the foot in under pressure. too tight does not allow you to push the aft spinnaker tape towards the hatch and collapse the spinnaker completely; the belly of the spinnaker will likely drop in the water

➤ bowperson and mast person are on opposite sides of the hatch to see and collect portions of the chute from all sides and shove it into the hatch

➤ keep the spinnaker up and full as long as possible if there is light wind

➤ be outside the jib ready to grab the spinnaker (if applicable)

➤ during the rounding, try to look forward and make sure you are not going to hit another boat. call any overlap (15. <u>[part of] watch for hazards</u>)

6. depower, collapse, and takedown the spinnaker

➢ grab the foot of the spinnaker when the cockpit follows the call to "blow the sheet." push the sail toward the hatch and pull the front of the foot in until you get to the clew. this keeps the spinnaker from dropping in front of the boat or overboard

➢ either you or mast grab the aft spinnaker tape, collapsing the spinnaker while collecting it and pushing it into the hatch

➢ the key is getting the two clews close together and the spinnaker not full

➢ after the spinnaker is collapsed and ready to go down the hatch call "halyard" and pull the head down

7. get the spinnaker in the hatch (not catching wind)

➢ assist mast and/or squirrel with getting the spinnaker in the hatch

➢ ensure that squirrel is not pulling anything into the hatch they are not supposed to. they are only supposed to stay below the hatch and grab whatever is handed to them or whatever comes in. the spinnaker goes under the pole before going in the hatch. the jib sheets and topping lift should not be wrapped in spinnaker or going down the hatch

➢ usually your next set will be a hatch set. I like to put the foot on the bottom and head on top where it is easy see the spinnaker triangle having no wraps before and during the hoist. mast and squirrel should be able to help with this

➢ all spinnaker sheets and afterguys slack gets thrown outside the hatch

➢ skirt the jib if needed

➢ when the sail is mostly down the hatch, send mast up to the rail

➢ all clews stay outside the hatch unless they need to be pulled down to clear any spinnaker wraps

➢ close the hatch as soon as possible. lower the butt of the pole when the spinnaker is down all the way and the hatch is closed

➢ the more sheets, afterguys, topping lifts, foreguy, and halyards that can stay attached, the better the probability for a clean set the next time

➢ duck under the jib and make sure the jib sheets come across cleanly (if applicable)

➢ 8. stay out of the way of the tacking or gybing boom

➢ 9. round the mark

➢ skirt the jib as cockpit 10. grind[s] the jib into position

➢ do only minimal cleanup to keep lines from dragging in the water or items to impede a tack

➢ 11. <u>prepare for tack</u>. make sure you are ready to tack shortly after takedown and call "ready to tack" a couple times

➢ 12. <u>distribute [your] weight properly</u>, usually you head to the rail as soon as possible

13. reset for another spinnaker set

➢ wait until the boat is up to speed and everyone else is on the rail, ask tactician if you can go on the bow

➢ make sure to ask squirrel if they ran the spinnaker tapes and cleaned the spinnaker. usually you have a feeling whether things came down cleanly or not. you can usually look into the hatch and see the spinnaker is laid out cleanly. if you or squirrel are not confident, you need to make sure the spinnaker is clean yourself. I am able to run the spinnaker from partially on the rail

➢ 14. <u>make sure nothing is dragging in the water</u>

➢ 15. <u>watch for hazards</u>

** if reaching and not able to square the pole back you can do a 'letterbox' takedown. bow team shall route the lazy sheet through the slot between the main sail and the boom. release the sheet on the windward side the pole was on. count down out loud and spike that side afterguy. releasing it will make the spinnaker fly loose to be taken down into the cockpit and pit hatch by others

Mast

1. coordinate in advance

o with bow telling you the order of the sequence and who does what

o ensure you know what squirrel is to do and not do

o ensure squirrel knows what to do and gets into position

2. prepare for the spinnaker takedown

o if you help with the hatch opening. call out "hatch open." do not to trap the sheets. always know where the hatch is on the boat to keep from falling into the hole

o if you have sheets and afterguys, you can grab the afterguy on the side of takedown. lead it under the jib and spinnaker pole. hand it down the hatch to the squirrel to pull on during the takedown

o jump the halyard to 3. raise the jib

o make sure the skipper turns down to 4. square the pole back prior to trip if previously on a reach ** o help with the pole stowing. Leave the butt end of the pole up a little to allow the spinnaker under it (5. remove and store the pole)

6. depower, collapse, and takedown the spinnaker

o grab the afterguy and pull with the squirrel and bow to get the spinnaker around the headstay if applicable and onto the deck near the hatch

o hand the clew and/or foot to the squirrel to pull down the hatch. squirrel should not reach out and grab the sail. everything should be handed to them first. then pulled down with an afterguy or tape attached to it

o either you or bow grab the aft spinnaker tape, collapsing the spinnaker while collecting it and pushing it into the hatch

o shove the clew and/or foot toward the hatch under the pole and jib and not wrapping the jib sheets

o make sure bow has collected the foot, assist if needed

o pull down on one of the sail tapes to get the halyard down

7. get the spinnaker in the hatch (not catching wind)

o ensure that squirrel is not pulling anything into the hatch they are not supposed to. they are only supposed to stay below the hatch and grab whatever is handed to them or whatever comes in. the spinnaker goes under the pole before going in the hatch. the jib sheets and topping lift should not be wrapped in spinnaker or going down the hatch

o stuff as much sail into the hatch as possible

o make sure the jib sheets are not wrapped in the spinnaker

o usually the next set will be a hatch set. I like to put the foot on the bottom and head on top where it is to easy see the spinnaker triangle having no wraps before and during the hoist. you and squirrel should be able to help with this

o duck under the jib and make sure the jib sheets come across cleanly (if applicable)

o 8. stay out of the way of the tacking or gybing boom

o 9. round the mark

o skirt the jib if needed while 10. [cockpit grinds] the jib into position

o help haul in the main sheet if it runs into the boom at the mast

o 12. distribute [your] weight properly, usually you head to the rail as soon as possible

Spin

** if reaching and not able to square the pole back the team can do a 'letterbox' takedown. bow team will route the lazy sheet through the slot between the main sail and the boom. bow will release the sheet on the windward side the pole was on. bow will count down out loud and spike that side afterguy. releasing it will make the spinnaker fly loose for pit, you and cockpit to take it down into the cockpit and pit hatch. pulling down at first on the lazy sheet already run through the letterbox

Pit

1. coordinate in advance

• if anybody is on deck forward of pit you are in charge of watching them and assisting with everything they may need. keep your eyes forward as much as possible. any amount of time looking down, looking at the cockpit, or looking elsewhere, means longer response time for things the person on the bow needs. more time before responses can mean more pulling or holding of something under load by the person on the bow; it always means more energy consumption just from standing on a usually tilted and bouncing bow. it is also a safety thing

• work with main trimmer to get boom vang, outhaul and cunningham set properly if applicable

• if you are doing end for end pole and which leeward buoy is not yet known, bow can unhook the foreguy to allow the jib to be raised in case another gybe happens. this will keep the jib from being trapped. you will no longer be able to lower the pole with the foreguy

• if you are gybing close to the mark, bow may mention doing a poleless gybe. bow will not hook up or raise the pole during the gybe. the pole will be stowed early

2. prepare for the spinnaker takedown

• make sure the spinnaker halyard is still clear and ready to be dropped

• close the jib cam cleat and wrap around a winch before hoisting

• 3. raise the jib and make sure it is ground up to its tension mark with enough time to do your other tasks, or have someone assist

• make sure the skipper turns down to 4. square the pole back prior to trip if previously on a reach **

• 5. remove and store the pole. lower the topping lift a bit quickly to trip the lines from the jaws. release it completely when bow has it to help get the pole stowed

6. depower, collapse, and takedown the spinnaker

• when bow is working their way along the foot of the spinnaker drop the halyard 5-10 feet to collapse the spinnaker and stop and wait for bow to haul in the slack. always have a wrap or two on a winch. keep your fingers clear. you can also use the cam cleat to do this

- only drop the rest of the halyard after the spinnaker is fully collapsed and the foot is at the hatch. take the halyard off the winch. usually bow calls "halyard" at this time. usually the halyard can be completely blown, but keep a watch and be ready to stop lowering again if needed. feed the line to the other side of the cam cleat if needed to help bow drop quickly. less pulling required by the bowperson means more conserved energy. getting the spinnaker down quickly allows for it to not be filled with air and allows the bowperson to get off the bow

- 8. <u>stay out of the way of the tacking or gybing boom</u>

- 12. <u>distribute [your] weight properly</u>, usually you head to the rail as soon as possible

** if reaching and not able to square the pole back, the team can do a 'letterbox' takedown. bow team will route the lazy sheet through the slot between the main sail and the boom. bow will release the sheet on the windward side the pole was on. bow will countdown out loud and spike that side afterguy. releasing it will make the spinnaker fly loose for you, mast and cockpit will to take it down into the cockpit and pit hatch, pulling down at first on the lazy sheet already run through the letterbox

Cockpit

<u>1. coordinate in advance</u>   &

<u>2. prepare for the spinnaker takedown</u>

◇ listen to what procedure the bow is going to do for takedown and ask questions if needed

◇ coordinate who is does what

◇ if you are doing end for end pole and which leeward buoy is not yet known, bow can unhook the foreguy to allow the jib to be raised in case another gybe happens. this will keep the jib from being trapped. a human guy may help. or 'tweakers' may work to hold the spinnaker down. or you may have to strap the spinnaker

◇ if you are gybing close to the mark, bow may mention doing a poleless gybe. bow will not hook up or raise the pole during the gybe. the pole will be stowed early

◇ always listen for people calling out for assistance needed

◇ always keep an eye forward when pulling or releasing something

◇ lock off the jib until the spinnaker is going down the hatch on takedown. this can be done with an alligator cleat or a hobbler. this keeps it from going in front of the headstay and blocking the takedown

Spin

◇ make sure the skipper turns down to 4. square the pole back prior to trip if previously on a reach **

   5. [bow removes and stores] the pole

◇ free-fly the spinnaker when the pole is removed (details in either of the gybe chapters prior: end for end, or dip pole)

◇ know what human guy does

◇ make sure someone has human guy on the sheet when the pole is removed

   6. depower, collapse, and takedown the spinnaker

◇ blow the sheet on the opposite side of the takedown to allow the spinnaker to flap in the wind when the call is made to "blow the sheet." make sure there is still a slight bit of tension on it. this allows the chute not to be loaded not out too far away from the boat. it also prevents the spinnaker from dropping in front of the bow or in the water on either side. ease it when bow is pulling the spinnaker down the hatch

◇ pull the sheet on the side of the takedown until the clew is at the pit to help get the spinnaker around the headstay (if applicable) and the foot on the deck. the bowperson cannot depower the spinnaker while getting the foot on the deck if the sail is full of air too far out, or if the foot is too strapped. ease it when bow is pulling the spinnaker down the hatch

◇ 8. stay out of the way of the tacking or gybing boom

◇ 9. round the mark

◇ 10. grind the jib into position

◇ 11. prepare for tack by wrapping the lazy winch and putting the handle in. leave slack to not hurt the jib. make sure the sheet is on the winch the correct way

◇ 12. distribute [your] weight properly, usually you head to the rail as soon as possible

◇ 13. [help bow] reset for another spinnaker set

◇ 14. make sure nothing is dragging in the water

** if reaching and not able to square the pole back, the team can do a 'letterbox' takedown. bow team will route the lazy sheet through the slot between the main sail and the boom. bow will release the sheet on the windward side the pole was on. bow will count down out loud and spike that side afterguy. releasing it will make the spinnaker fly loose for pit, mast and you will take it down into the cockpit and pit hatch, pulling down at first on the lazy sheet already run through the letterbox

Main Trim

1. coordinate in advance

❖ get someone to assist with grinding in the main. or help with hauling it in if runs into the boom at the mast

❖ make sure outhaul, cunningham, and boom vang are set properly

❖ watch forward for any obstacles because the bowperson is busy: boats, kelp, obstructions, etc. (15. watch for hazards)

❖ make sure everyone 4. stay[s] out of the way of the tacking or gybing boom and main sheet

❖ watch forward to call out if there are any issues with the takedown

Skipper

☐ turn down to 4. square the pole back prior to trip if previously on a reach

☐ drive as close to DDW as possible until the spinnaker is 2/3rds of the way in the hatch. even if it means driving past the mark a little (6. depower, collapse, and takedown the spinnaker)

☐ 8. stay out of the way of the tacking or gybing boom

☐ 9. round the mark

☐ 13. watch for hazards [ahead only]

Tactician

1. coordinate in advance

♪ notify bow which gybe you will be on and which mark will be rounded in advance

♪ try to do the same type of rounding consistently to which the team is accustomed

♪ ensure bow has covered the takedown procedure

♪ ensure the jib will not be trapped

♪ advise in advance if you are deciding to tack quickly after the takedown

♪ call out to other boats if they need to know the rules based on your position (15. [part of] watch for hazards)

♪ 2. [make sure they] prepare for the spinnaker takedown

Spin

♪ 3. [make sure they] raise the jib

♪ make sure the skipper turns down to 4. square the pole back prior to trip if previously on a reach

♪ call a cadence sequence to perform the tasks during the takedown: stow the pole, human guy, raise the jib, blow the sheet, turn the boat

♪ 5. [make sure they] remove and store the pole

♪ 6. [make sure they] depower, collapse, and takedown the spinnaker

♪ 7. [make sure they] get the spinnaker in the hatch (not catching wind)

♪ 8. [make sure everyone stays] out of the way of the tacking or gybing boom

♪ 9. round the mark

♪ 10. [make sure they] grind the jib into position

♪ 11. [make sure they] prepare for tack

♪ 12. [coordinate how to] distribute weight properly

♪ 13. [make sure they] reset for another spinnaker set

♪ 14. make sure nothing is dragging in the water

♪ 15. watch for hazards

** if reaching and not able to square the pole back, the team can do a 'letterbox' takedown. bow team will route the lazy sheet through the slot between the main sail and the boom. bow will release the sheet on the windward side the pole was on. bow will count down out loud and spike that side afterguy. releasing it will make the spinnaker fly loose for pit, mast and you will take it down into the cockpit and pit hatch, pulling down at first on the lazy sheet already run through the letterbox

See Chapter 5 Upwind next if doing another lap

See Chapter 4 Prestart & Start next if starting a new race

Spin

Bow requires a three-dimensional recall and vision of how things are and how they are going to be. It requires being aware of things all over the boat. Being on a sideways and bouncing deck while using your hands to do things, usually above your head. Doing their job while trying not to fall or get pushed, pulled, wrapped, hit, thrown, etc....

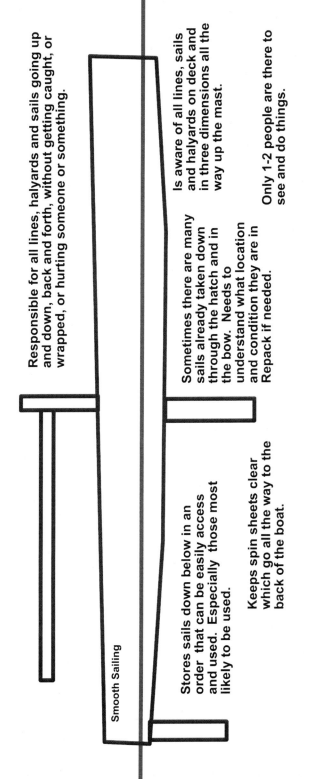

Responsible for all lines, halyards and sails going up and down, back and forth, without getting caught, or wrapped, or hurting someone or something.

Sometimes there are many sails already taken down through the hatch and in the bow. Needs to understand what location and condition they are in. Repack if needed.

Is aware of all lines, sails and halyards on deck and in three dimensions all the way up the mast.

Only 1-2 people are there to see and do things.

Smooth Sailing

Stores sails down below in an order that can be easily access and used. Especially those most likely to be used.

Keeps spin sheets clear which go all the way to the back of the boat.

Cockpit

Eyes forward when pulling on anything watching how it affects the front.

Always listen for information being called out to change something to assist with a situation.

Pit (part of the bow team)

Eyes forward whenever anyone is in front of the mast. Help release or snug things. The longer someone is on the bow the more tired they get. Also safer having someone watching in case falls overboard or gets hurt.

Relay information back and forth.

Everyone helps bow and mast with what they can. Especially resetting the boat before and after races.

Get this and more free resources to share and use at my website

www.TeamCoordinatedRacing.com